Himmler

Himmler

Alan Wykes

BB

Editor-in-Chief: Barrie Pitt
Editor: David Mason
Art Director: Sarah Kingham
Picture Editor: Robert Hunt
Consultant Art Editor: Dennis Piper
Designer: Michael Frost
Illustration: John Batchelor
Photographic Research: Carina Dvorak
Cartographer: Richard Natkiel

Photographs for this book were especially selected from the following archives; from left to right page 3 Keystone Press Agency, London; 4 Rijksinstituut voon Oonlogsdocumentatie, Amsterdam; 4 US National Archives; 4 US Archives; 4 Rijksinstituut; 4 US Archives; 8 Keystone; 9 Bundesarchiv, Koblenz; 10 US Archives; 11 Suddeutscher Verlag, Munchen; 12-15 Czech News Agency, Praha; 16 Staatsbibliothek, Berlin; 17 Czech; 18 Bundesarchiv; 20 Archiv Gerstenberg, Germany; 22 Suddeutscher; 23-24 Bundesarchiv; 24-25 Novosti Press Agency, London; 26 Bundesarchiv; 27 Gerstenberg; 28 Suddeutscher; 29 Bundesarchiv; 30 Suddeutscher; 30 Zeitgeschictliches Bildarchiv, Munchen; 30 Bundesarchiv; 30-32 US Archives; 33 US Library of Congress; 34-35 US Archives; 36-37 Library of Congress; 38-39 US Archives; 40 Suddeutscher; 40 Library of Congress; 42-43 Suddeutscher; 44 US Archives; 45 Staatsbib; 46 Gerstenberg; 47 US Archives; 49 Ullstein GmbH, Berlin; 50 Bundesarchiv; 51 Suddeutscher; 52 Ullstein; 53 US Archives; 54 Suddeutscher; 54-55 Zeitgeschichtliches; 56 Staatsbib; 57 US Archives; 58 Gerstenberg; 59 Bundesarchiv; 60 Suddeutscher; 60-61 Ullstein; 60-62 Suddeutscher; 62-63 Bundesarchiv; 63 Suddeutscher; 64-65 Bundesarchiv; 66 US Archives; 69 Bundesarchiv; 70 Ullstein; 71 Suddeutscher; 72-73 Staatsbib; 74 Ullstein; 75-76 US Archives; 77 Ullstein; 78-82 Suddeutscher; 82 US Archives; 83 Ullstein; 84 Bundesarchiv; 85 Gerstenberg; 86 Ullstein; 87 Suddeutscher; 88 Gerstenberg; 89 Dr A Bernfes, London; 90-91 Suddeutscher; 92-94 US Archives; 95 Keystone; 96-97 Staatsbib; 98 US Archives; 99 Staatsbib; 100 Ullstein; 100-101 Ullstein; 100-101 US Archives; 102 Suddeutscher; 103 Ullstein; 104 Suddeutscher; 106-107 Bundesarchiv; 108 US Archives; 109 Bernfes; 110 US Archives; 112-113 Bundesarchiv; 114 Ullstein; 115 Bernfes; 116 Keystone; 117 Bundesarchiv; 118-119 US Archives; 119 Ullstein; 120 US Archives; 121 Bundesarchiv; 121 Ullstein; 122-123 Bundesarchiv; 124-127 Suddeutscher; 128 Library of Congress; 130 Suddeutscher; 131 US Archives; 131 Imperial War Museum, London; 132-133 Suddeutscher; 134 Gerstenberg; 135 Suddeutscher; 135 Ullstein; 136 Suddeutscher; 137 Gerstenberg; 138-139 Library of Congress; 140 Ullstein; 141 Suddeutscher; 142 Bundesarchiv; 143-144 Staatsbib; 145 Suddeutscher; 146 Staatsbib; 147 Czech; 148-149 Staatsbib; 150 Czech; 151 Bundesarchiv; 152 Ullstein; 153 Suddeutscher; 154 Gerstenberg; 156 Suddeutscher; 157-158 US Archives; 159 Ullstein; Front cover US National Archives; Back cover US National Archives

First Printing: July 1972
Printed in United States of America

Ballantine Books Inc.
101 Fifth Avenue New York NY 10003

An Intext Publisher

Contents

The career of a filing clerk

Introduction by Barrie Pitt

On 4th May 1945, the German surrender was signed at Montgomery's headquarters on Luneberg Heath. This simple ceremony marked the end of the Third Reich, created by Adolf Hitler to last for a thousand years; although from the time of his appointment as Chancellor on 30th January 1933 until his death in the Chancellory bunker in the ruins of the German capital, only twelve years had elapsed.

Twelve years is but the merest fragment of time when measured against the history of mankind – a history full of war and violence, of intolerance and racial hatred. But even in the context of history as defined by Winston Churchill – 'a catalogue of the crimes and stupidities of mankind' – those twelve years of preparation for and prosecution of a war for world domination plumbed the depths of human suffering. Men, women and children, both inside and outside Germany, learned the sinister connotations of words like 'Gestapo' and 'concentration camp' and found that harmless-sounding groups of initials – SA, SD, and SS – hid the identities of grim instruments of power with which the Nazis enforced their political philosophy. At their head sat Heinrich Himmler.

Surrounding Adolf Hitler was a court of sycophants and toadies, men who jostled one another for shares in the spoils of power and who administered the grotesque state that Germany became, dominated by the overriding will of their leader. Göring, Goebbels, and Heinrich Himmler were the personalities who stood out among this new German aristocracy, and of the three it was Himmler who eventually wielded most real power and was entrusted by Hitler with the practical application of his racial policy.

Born in Bavaria in 1900 into a highly respected Catholic family, Himmler was named after Prince Heinrich of Bavaria to whom his father had been tutor. Despite his physical weakness he was an ardent admirer of the German army and had been an officer cadet at the conclusion of the First World War. As a 'first generation' member of the Nazi Party, he was present at the unsuccessful Munich 'putsch' of 1923, which resulted in Hitler being sent to prison for treason and Himmler losing his job as salesman with a firm of fertiliser manufacturers, for taking time off without permission.

His was a personality with a marked tendency towards hero-worship, and although in those early days there is little evidence that he was close to the Führer, he conceived a passionate loyalty to both Hitler and Ernst Röhm, leader of the SA. In 1925 this loyalty was rewarded for he became 'deputy district leader of the party', and at the same time was given the apparently insignificant post of second-in-command of the SS. At that time, the SS was only a small inner group of the powerful SA – but it was to expand into a far stronger group than the parent body, and in 1934 as a result of the 'Night of the Long Knives' it was to commit a form of patricide as the instrument of Röhm's death, thus neutralising and emasculating the powers of the once all-powerful Brownshirts, and indeed. taking that power to themselves.

Thus it was almost by chance that Himmler became one of the Nazi élite. Without a thirst for personal power (for he was always the devoted follower) he nevertheless loved the high-flown titles he was given and he diligently applied his peculiar talents to the furtherance of Nazi ideals. He was an indefatigable filer of facts. Even as an orderly-room corporal in the army he had noted confidential information concerning his comrades, and now his passion for accumulating damaging knowledge of other people's indiscretions and hidden weaknesses was given free rein. In his steel filing cabinets the confidential dossiers multiplied and waxed fat, stuffed full of carefully garnered minutiae which, in the hands of the Reichsführer-SS could result in death or imprisonment for those unfortunate enough to be of interest to him.

As head of the SS Intelligence (SD) Himmler appointed Reinhard Heydrich, a man with the physical attributes which he himself lacked. Heydrich carried out, as Himmler's *alter ego*, those tasks for which the Reichsführer-SS was unsuited, leaving him free for researching his racialist theories, drawing up the 'Clan Book of the SS' and formulating his marriage laws for maintaining the purity of the Nordic blood.

By April 1934, all police and security departments including the sinister *Geheimes Staats Polizei* – better known as the Gestapo – were placed by Hitler under Himmler's command, as were the concentration camps inaugurated by Hermann Göring in 1933. Under Himmler's control the name was to become synonomous with torture, starvation, and death; they formed part of the 'final solution' for European Jews, and after 1941 the crematorium chimneys at Dachau, Auschwitz, and numerous other camps belched smoke as the bodies of over 10,000,000 people done to death within their grim confines were clinically disposed of.

So great were the numbers of people put to death by Himmler and his subordinates that the figures become meaningless – mere cold statistics; it needs an effort of will for a rational person to accept the fact that Heydrich, when appointed Protector of Bohemia-Moravia — Hitler's name for Czechoslovakia – declared it his policy completely to exterminate the 30,000,000 Slavs and Jews of Eastern Europe.

Neither Heydrich nor Himmler stood trial at Nuremburg, Heydrich dying in 1942 of wounds received from an assassin's grenade, Himmler in captivity when he bit into a cyanide capsule concealed in his mouth. They were evil men – the one ruthlessly pursuing power and personal aggrandisement, the other full of gimcrack theories concerning the superiority of the Nordic races. Such men exist in many societies and manage to live comparatively ordinary lives - or at worst become petty criminals – but nurtured by the political philosophy of Nazism the dreadful potentialities of Himmler and Heydrich burgeoned, and between them they created the largest instrument for mass terror the world has ever known.

The grand inquisitor

Upon the city of Prague with its many spires and turrets and towers snow began to fall early in the morning of 15th December 1941. It fell slowly and weightlessly like feathers shaken from the heavy bed of cloud that lay over the city. There was no wind to drift it, and by mid-morning it was no more than a spindrift that was smutched by the traffic into black intricate designs like the scribblings of a child in heavy black pencil.

In the square before the cathedral a space had been cordoned off with rope coloured red, black and white. The cordon was slung from thin iron uprights poking up from heavy bases. Each upright was surmounted by a medallion the size of a dinner plate on which was embossed the eagle and swastika of the German Third Reich. The space thus enclosed was rectangular in shape, one of its long sides of about 100 yards being parallel with the west front of the cathedral. Along that side of the rectangle, and outside the tricolour cordon, a number of yellow discs had been painted on the concourse; there were in fact 100 of

them; and since daylight an old man with a withered arm had been engaged in sweeping the snow from them as it fell. His foreman in the Highways Department had told him that on no account was snow to be allowed to cover the discs, which were 'of vital importance to the ceremony'.

On the opposite long side of the rectangle, and also outside the cordon, a machine gun pointing toward the cathedral was mounted on a low daïs. Behind the gun a sandbag had been placed on the daïs where the gunner was to kneel. Farther back still a small pavilion had been built of wood and canvas. It contained five heavy carved chairs which stood in an orderly line awaiting occupants who would in due course be the audience for the spectacle that had been arranged.

Setting aside the machine gun, the scene had about it something almost

Prague: Nazi parade in the Cathedral square where Himmler witnessed the execution of one hundred citizens accused of attempting to 'subvert the regime'

of gaiety, of Christmas card festivity. The Nazi flags that decorated the pavilion hung motionless round their masts. Now and again the sweeper rested his besom against one of the upright cordon supports, walked round the rectangle and shook the light powdering of snow from the flags, then returned to his task of sweeping the discs. In the distance the rumble of the trams could be heard, and, very faintly, the organist in the cathedral practising a passage from a Handel concerto. At all the approaches to the concourse pairs of sentries paced up and down, occasionally banging their arms across their bodies against the cold.

It was Obergruppenführer-SS Kurt Schact-Isserlis, the man in charge of the arrangements for the morning, who remembered these and many other details and recorded them in rough notes which in due course fell into the hands of Allied Intelligence officers when he became a prisoner of war.

It was no new task for Schact-Isserlis to arrange an execution. He was meticulous in his attention to detail and timing and had a sense of drama which he invariably indulged, but for which this morning he would have a distinguished – and, he hoped, appreciative – audience: Reichsführer-SS Heinrich Himmler and Reinhard Tristan Eugen Heydrich, who had recently been appointed 'Protector' of Bohemia-Moravia.

Schact-Isserlis was a square-faced man with thick blond wavy hair, a

sensual and slightly lopsided mouth, a rather heavy nose, and small neat ears. A duelling scar ran from the corner of his right eye down to his jawbone. He was thirty-three and came from Fallersleben, Thuringia.

At 11.45 he dismissed the sweeper, crossed to the pavilion and made sure everything was in order there, then walked quickly with his hands linked behind his back to the guardroom on the south side of the concourse. There he ordered the sergeant of the guard to fall his men in as the guard of honour for the visitors and 'proceed with the arrangements'.

The sergeant's commands rang out and the sentries instantly snapped into the formal movements of assembly and lined up in two ranks facing each other across the main approach road. Almost at once two outriders on motorcycles arrived. They were followed by two Mercedes open tourers carrying Himmler and Heydrich with Konrad Henlein, Head of Civil Administration, and Hans Frank, Chief of Police. The two cars drove straight to the pavilion, where the passengers were welcomed by Schact-Isserlis with Nazi salutes. All took their seats in the pavilion, Schact-Isserlis shifting his chair slightly behind the others in deference to their rank.

At noon precisely – a series of clocks could be heard striking over the city – the door of the guardroom opened and the long column of those about to die emerged. The condemned were led and flanked by guards with machine car-

Far left: Reinhard Heydrich, appointed 'Protector' of Bohemia Moravia, also present at the execution ceremony. *Left:* Konrad Henlein, Head of Civilian Administration in Prague. *Right:* Chief of Police, Hans Frank

The Führer inspects his army of occupation in the Czechoslovakian capital, 1939

bines. They were ordinary people – a cross-section of those that might pass any street corner in a big town during a day. The relevant dossiers – for naturally they all had dossiers that had found their way via the Gestapo into Himmler's filing cabinets – revealed that they were clerks, students, housewives, labourers – the usual motley of any urban civilization. The oldest among them was seventy-four, the youngest seventeen. Their common crime was that they had, in one way or another, 'attempted to subvert the régime'. Their alleged subversive words had been picked up by hidden microphones and recorded, and when played back at their 'trial' had been found susceptible to much devious twisting.

The collection and collation of the 'evidence' against them had gone on for some fifteen months. Hitler had marched into Czechoslovakia on 13th March 1939, from which moment that

Right: **The conquerors march through Prague.** **Below:** **Prague's citizenry show their detestation of the Nazis**

compilation of states had, according to the Führer, ceased to exist. Instead, he offered the world the Protectorate of Bohemia-Moravia, thus simultaneously giving Chamberlain a convenient opportunity of disregarding the British guarantee against aggression given to Czechoslovakia, and rewarding Hungary for her pro-Nazi activities with the payoff of the eastern tip of Czechoslovakia, hitherto Ruthenia. But the régime had been too frailly established to permit of any risk of subversion. Under Hitler's direction steps were taken 'to ensure that an example is made of the few agitators who would throw away their new-found freedom in a futile attempt to resist the Third Reich'.

The resisters of the Third Reich were too shrewd, in Czechoslovakia as elsewhere to 'agitate' in any blatant manner. So it was by no means simple to collect evidence against them. The difficulty of getting such evidence, however, did not deter the Gestapo, who were well trained in patience by Reichsführer-SS Himmler. So fifteen months later, in June 1940,

enough had been pieced together to 'justify' the arrest of 100 people who had been tried and been found guilty of subversive acts against the state. Their execution, about to take place, was therefore an exemplary one. No-

one, the theory ran, would henceforth be so foolish as to risk such an outcome to their indiscretions.

The prisoners were now standing, one on each yellow disc, facing the distinguished audience across the cordoned space. The guards had divided and withdrawn, in a series of precise drill movements, to the short sides of the rectangle and to the ends

Head of the Gestapo, Heinrich Himmler. A British view of Himmler, reproduced in *Le Journal*

HIMMLER, chef de la Gestapo

(D'après un dessin de ZEC, paru dans « The Daily Mirror »)

and rear of the rank of prisoners, from which vantage points they kept their charges covered with their carbines. A hundred prisoners attempting a mass escape was improbable; but the Waffen-SS was there to cope with improbabilities.

There was no attempt at escape. 'Their faces were indistinct from the pavilion,' Schact-Isserlis recalled.

'There were two old women with shawls over their heads, and some young girls wearing men's boots. The men had caps with earflaps and peaks, there was one man with a *steifer Filzhut* [bowler] also several *weicher*

Some of the victims of the hunt for subversive elements rounded up on the Nazi takeover

[Hombergs]. Some were bare-headed, many had no coats, but they were going to die in a moment, warmth was of little account to them. They were just a row of skittles, faces. I had a list of all their names neatly typed, pasted to a board and varnished over, the varnish to prevent the names being smudged if it was raining and in case the Reichsführer wanted a roll called. He didn't, though. Heydrich signalled to me to carry on and I gave the order to the guard sergeant.'

The executioner was escorted from the guardroom and took his place behind the machine gun on the daïs. His greatcoat was draped over his shoulders like a cape. He had a swaggering walk and seemed to be well aware that he was the star performer in the drama. Kneeling behind the gun he looked over his shoulder once, then grasped the grips of the gun and awaited the order to fire.

The guards now moved off in groups. With their carbines slung over their shoulders, they marched briskly back to the guardroom and filed into it. Inside, they crowded round the windows with their faces pressed to the glass. 'One thought of children looking wonderingly out on the world of Santa Klaus,' Schact-Isserlis wrote. 'They rubbed the frost and breath away from the windows with their sleeves and waited for the puppet show to begin.'

Reinhard Heydrich with Heinrich Himmler at the Berlin Sports Arena in 1941

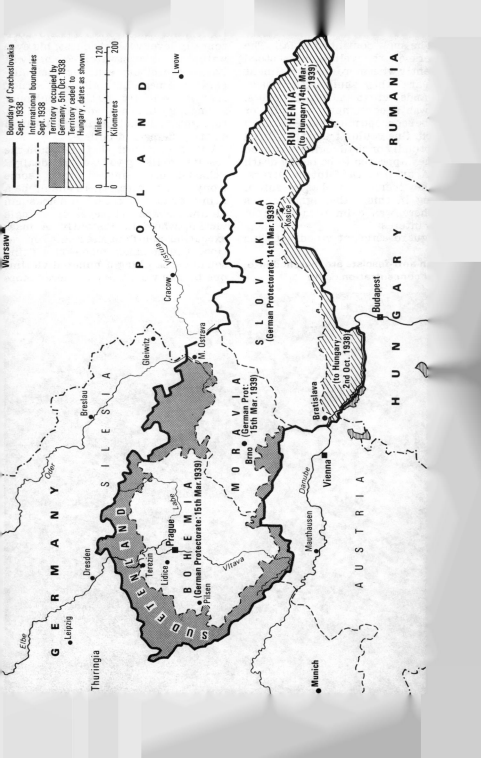

It was now a few minutes before 12.15. The snow continued to fall. The prisoners on the yellow discs stood 'apparently with more embarrassment than fear – they shuffled their feet, their hands were in and out of pockets, there was a contemptuous smile or two to be seen, one middle-aged woman coughed. One couldn't say they faced death proudly or challengingly or even that they appeared to be facing death at all. Apart from the faint embarrassment they seemed to feel as a result of standing in this rather ignominious row, there was calm detachment – almost interest.'

The guard sergeant stood with his

Sudeten anti-fascists are marched into Dachau concentration camp

right hand raised, his left held horizontally level with his chest, his eyes watching his wristwatch. Precisely at 12.15 – the clocks sounded their disparate chimes – his right hand struck sharply downward and the executioner swung his gun in a steady arc from left to right and back again, the barrel spitting flame and bullets.

With such a method of execution the results are likely to be ugly. 'Ideally,' Schact-Isserlis mused with some irony in his notes, 'there should be a firing squad of six, each a marksman aiming between the eyes of a single victim, who falls instantly. A mass execution calls for a less refined operation. The demands made on a firing squad despatching a hundred victims one by one would be considered more

than the call of duty imposed upon them. They might become wearied; their shoulders would certainly become bruised by the repeated recoil of their rifles. There might be complaints to the Welfare Officer, there could even be mutinous undertones. A speedier method is called for, and the machine gun is the answer – but an answer that brings with it the crudities of mechanisation.'

So it was in this case. The gunner's arc of fire was too sweeping, the mechanism of his weapon too rapid, for such finesse as a posse of marksmen could have brought to the task. The spray of bullets pierced heads, chests, abdomens, limbs. A number of the victims toppled immediately as the gun raked from left to right, mercifully and instantaneously despatched; a number more fell on the return sweep. Then the gunner paused. Perhaps the pause formed part of his orders; perhaps he was a man who liked to observe the effects of agony. It cannot now be ascertained. At all events, he paused and observed the result of his handiwork.

It was a horrifying sight – a compound of all that Goya, Bosch and Doré might have portrayed pictorially. Something like two-thirds of the victims had fallen, but clearly not all were dead for some were clawing at their clothes and shrieking or moving among the inert bodies of those killed instantly. The remaining third were grotesques with agonized faces spurting gouts of blood, hands clutching at torn flesh, limbs moving in puppet gestures in a skirmish of horror. 'The gunner in his pause seemed to be dispassionately considering whether he would rake the victims with his fire again; but at that moment there came a distraction.'

The distraction was in the pavilion. Schact-Isserlis, sitting slightly behind Himmler, was aware that the Reichsführer had slumped in his highbacked chair. One of his hands fell lifelessly over the arm. Beside Himmler, Heydrich looked curiously for a moment at the chalk-white face, the rimless glasses slightly askew, the lips drawn back from the teeth. Schact-Isserlis says Heydrich's interest was momentarily torn between the scene at the far end of the cordoned space and the Grand Inquisitor who had fainted at the sight of the execution he had commanded. 'There was a look of contempt on Heydrich's face. Together with the Chief of Police he caught at Himmler's shoulders and thrust his head down between his knees. His glasses fell off and the clicking sound they made on the floor was simultaneous with the sound of the machine gun as the executioner swept his gun from left to right again, from right to left. . . .'

This time there were no writhing bodies left. The executioner, more by merciful fortune than accurate aim, had completed his task. The dead lay forming a long parapet beyond which the doors of the cathedral loomed. With precise timing two open five-ton trucks carrying two small squads of prisoners under guard now backed into the concourse. The multi-coloured cordon was lowered and the vehicles eased up against the human parapet. The two squads of prisoners, now set about slinging – no word would more aptly describe their action – the bodies into the truck. Each body landed with a faintly resonant thump on the iron floor. It was evident that the squad of prisoners were innured to such work. They probably came from one of the concentration camps where Jews were exterminated and to which they would equally probably return, to be exterminated in their turn.

Himmler had by now recovered to the extent of being able to stand unsteadily. He put out an arm toward Heydrich. 'Something to hold on to,' he said. It was a phrase that was to be remembered. He carefully avoided looking across the concourse, stepped down from the pavilion and climbed into the Mercedes. The resonant thudding of the bodies went on as he was driven away with Heydrich beside him.

Clerk in unholy orders

Himmler greets his Führer during the
Reichsparteitag parade in 1938

Heinrich Himmler's parents were very respectable people. The senior Himmler – his name was Gebhard – could claim eminence in his respectability. He had been tutor to one of the members of the Royal Bavarian court, Prince Heinrich, a descendant of the mad King Ludwig. With his royal connexions and a professorship from the University of Munich the obeisances of the neighbours could not have been more justly earned. The 'Herr Professor' and his wife and sons (there was an older son, also called Gebhard, and a younger, Ernst) were looked upon as examples of all that Bavarians should be.

Heinrich Himmler was a studious, prim child with a weak stomach and short sight. His elder brother records that he was 'kind to old ladies and often ran errands for them and carried their shopping.' His brain was not brilliant but he was a good deal brighter at school than Adolf Hitler was, and

The Himmler family in about 1905, Heinrich stands in front of his mother

certainly far more industrious.

He was also more amenable to discipline. In fact he appears to have looked in all directions for 'rules', apparently believing that if the rules were always followed success would result. A touching belief. He spent ten years trying to learn to play the piano, for which he had no talent at all, and was mystified because (as he records in his diary) 'the results are unmusical and inaccurate in spite of Professor Härtel's assurances that if the rule of slow practice is followed there must be achievement.'

Rules, however, made more sense in such subjects as mathematics, Latin and Greek, in all of which Himmler gained moderate markings on his school papers. But his real ambition

Left: Heinrich (posing far right) seems to be practising his future role! Discipline and inflexible rules of conduct early had a fascination for him. *Below:* Russians taken prisoner in 1915. Himmler concentrated much of his hatred on the Russians, for he had seen thousands of his wounded countrymen return from Russia during the First World War

was to join the army. There he knew he would find rules enough. His direction would be pointed from reveille to lights-out. It wasn't altogether that he lacked confidence and needed guidance, though he did to some extent. Rather, he found great satisfaction in the achievement of a task by methods that either existed or could be thought out.

The army offered more than exacting rules and a measure of nationalistic glory: it offered a war to fight in. Being unable to give his services to his country before he reached the regulation age of seventeen – and that was one rule he fretted at – he recorded in his diary many pious longings to 'get to the front and help to rid the world of the Russian vermin'. He appears to have singled out the Russians as particular objects of hatred mainly because Landshut, where the Himmlers lived during the years 1913 to 1919, was a transit camp for prisoners of war from the Eastern Front. It was a brash judgement rather than one inspired by malice such as Hitler's against 'the world of Bolsheviks and Jews', which the Austrian corporal brooded over during

his service on the Western Front. Unlike his future Führer, Himmler had no megalomaniac designs for setting the world on a different course.

From records of his childhood and youth, we glean a picture of a rather prissy youth, given to the study of philately and the enthusiastic use of dumb-bells to strengthen his muscles, anxious to please and full of courteous respect for his elders, a regular church-goer (the Himmlers, like the Hitlers, were Roman Catholics) and revealing a somewhat sentimental appreciation of the beauties of nature. Also in his diaries and letters (which are for the most part uninspired factual records of the weather, walks taken, appointments for tuition in fencing and the like), we find repeated references to the 'honourable and wholesome attitude to sex that should be the ideal of every true German'.

'I am determined to remain chaste until marriage, however much I might be tempted,' he wrote to his brother Gebhard; and went on sanctimoniously: 'A real man will love a woman in three ways: first, as a dear child who must be admonished, perhaps even punished when she is foolish, though she must also be protected and looked after because she is so weak; secondly, he will love her as his wife and loyal comrade, who helps him fight in the struggle of life, always at his side but never dampening his spirit. Thirdly, he will love her as his wife whose feet he longs to kiss and who gives him the strength never to falter even in the worst strife, the strength she gives him thanks to her childlike purity.'

There is in such utterances a superficial idealism that, in view of subsequent events, is as distasteful as his declaration, made in 1919, that 'Whatever happens I shall always love God and pray to Him, and remain faithful to the Catholic church and defend it even if I should be expelled from it.'

Himmler was motivated by the fanaticism of orderliness. If certain goals were to be achieved, he believed that any method, whatever side issues it involved, was justified. He was not overtly malevolent. As we shall see, he was capable of compassion though it was normally misdirected. Also, though he achieved leadership – fortuitously – he was designed for subordination. The child who wanted to please became the man whose greatest satisfaction lay in slavishness. In seeking that satisfaction he vacillated and clung like a leech to the ideas of others.

One of them was anti-Semitism, though he was not pathological about it like Hitler. Postwar Bavaria, particularly Munich, was, like prewar Vienna, rife with antipathy toward

Left: Elder brother Gebhard, recipient of numbers of lugubrious letters from Heinrich on German Ideals, the Proper Attitude to Women and other topics dear to his heart. **Right:** Students at Landshut, Himmler seated second from left, immediately before he joined the Munich Technical High School and University as an agriculture student in 1919

Judaism. The Catholic right-wing element was strong – a powerful and often vicious opponent of Freemasonry and what the extremist press called 'The insidious infiltration of world Jewry and its grasping attempts to control international finance and impoverish the people for its own wealth'. Himmler picked up these sentiments and they are scattered through his diaries and letters of the 1920s. 'Jew louse' and similar shallow insults are applied to duelling opponents, companions on supposedly healthy country walks, and fellow students at the Munich Technical High School and University, where he studied agriculture from 1919 until 1922. But one senses that there was little venom behind the insults, and little philosophical consideration either for that matter. Himmler, the man who sought direction, invariably made facile judgements.

The other influence he absorbed with far more positive enthusiasm was that of the army, once he got in it. He was called up and served in the 11th Bavarian Infantry Regiment for a little over a year, from 1917 to December 1918. Towards the end of that time he was an officer cadet, but the armistice came too soon for him to be commissioned and on his release he merely transferred to the local *Freikorps*, a band of furtively armed volunteers whose illegality he disapproved of, before seeking a commission in the Reichswehr – the regular army of 100,000 men permitted by the Versailles Treaty. He never gained his commission – an attack of paratyphoid laid him low and left him too weak to do anything but continue his studies in agriculture – but his fanatical regard for orders and orderliness found its anchorage in the drills and training programmes of the cadet school.

While in the army he also served a spell as an orderly room clerk, and in doing so became stimulated by the filing systems where reports on his fellow cadets were stored. 'Surprising,' he recorded, 'that Erich changed his name upon entering the service. Why, I wonder?' 'I noticed today that Kobbe served detention for insubordi-

nation'. 'In the 1915 cadre the sergeant-major was reduced to the ranks for pilfering and transferred to the Cleves Battalion.' 'I was quite pleased today to discover misfiled a transcript of a Court Martial in which a certain Lieutenant Müller received a sentence for grave sexual offences.'

Who these people were is irrelevant now. The importance of Himmler's interest in their records lies in the indication it gives us of his methodical pursuit of information that not only arouses his curiosity but, one feels, is information that he realises he could put to some use, given the necessity. The necessity was not to be held long in abeyance.

The political and economic situation in the Germany of the 1920s was complex and turbulent. The Weimar Republic, constituted in August 1919, was based on democratic principles and was established by the majority of an enormous electorate – 30,000,000 of the eligible 35,000,000 – after which it began its main task of setting up a constitution that would embrace the best features of British, American and Swiss government. Disunity was everywhere evident, however. The German National People's Party was stiff with Conservative monarchists who under the guise of 'renewing old and proven ideals' worked for the restoration of the Hohenzollern monarchy. Stresemann's ambiguously named German People's Party stood for Liberal ideals and a union with Austria (it had gained only five per cent of the seats in the Assembly). There was also a Christian People's Party (strongly Catholic), led by a man called Matthias Erzberger, which protested republican ideals and captured ninety seats. Majority Socialists (led by Friedrich Ebert) and Independent Socialists were parties with Leftist views who between them gained forty-six per cent of the seats; and the Democratic Party – vaguely monarchist and equally vaguely anti-militarist in its aims – surprisingly got control of forty per cent.

None of these parties had a working majority; but Ebert, having offered the Independent Socialists terms for collaboration which the Independents rejected, switched his alliance to the Democrats and Christians and thereby gained a majority of 331 for the three coalescing parties.

In spite of its initial constitutional success, the Weimar Republic was

Above: Minister of Finance Matthias Erzberger, who led the Christian People's Party. *Below:* Majority Socialist leader Friedrich Ebert. *Right:* The ranks of disillusioned German soldiery who returned in 1918 to the punitive strictures of the Versailles Treaty

buffeted from all sides for its defeatist acceptance of the terms of the Versailles Treaty. In Bavaria especially, turmoil reigned. A Communist régime that had briefly held power during the early months of 1919 was bloodily overthrown on 1st May by the *Reichswehr* and the *Freikorps* combined. The *Freikorps* thereupon attracted the disgruntled loyalties of (as William Shirer calls them) 'The great mob of demobilised soldiers for whom the bottom had fallen out of the world in 1918, uprooted men who could not find jobs or their way back to the peaceful society they had left in 1914, men grown tough and violent through war who could not shake themselves from ingrained habit and who, as Hitler, who for a while was one of

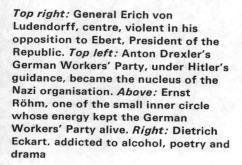

Top right: General Erich von Ludendorff, centre, violent in his opposition to Ebert, President of the Republic. *Top left:* Anton Drexler's German Workers' Party, under Hitler's guidance, became the nucleus of the Nazi organisation. *Above:* Ernst Röhm, one of the small inner circle whose energy kept the German Workers' Party alive. *Right:* Dietrich Eckart, addicted to alcohol, poetry and drama

them, would later say, "became revolutionaries who favoured revolution for its own sake and desired to see revolution established as a permanent condition".'

There were not only active revolutionaries but also many who disputed the eastern frontiers as designated by Versailles; there were freebooters, trade unionists who organised extensive strikes, Communist agitators . . . and General Erich Ludendorff, who nursed a bitter hatred of Ebert, the President of the Republic.

Also, in due course, there was Adolf Hitler.

Hitler, that pernicious advocate of the overthrow of the Weimar Republic – the 'November Criminals' as he called them – had become, of all improbable things, an Education Officer (*Bildungsoffizier*) in the political department of the Munich Command of the *Reichswehr*. The job had been given him in recognition of the value of an anti-Semitic outburst he had made at a *Reichswehr* school of 'political education' that had been set up to combat left-wing influences. He was still no more than a corporal, but rank was of no account to propagandists. He bludgeoned people into listening to the ceaseless flow of words he shouted in his harsh voice and accompanied by the gestures, pleas and rebukes that were to mesmerize millions into believing him a saviour.

In 1919 the masses of disillusioned, demobilised soldiers were prepared to listen to anyone, as the huge electorate that established the Republic proved; and numerous splinter groups sprang up, giving themselves names of typically Teutonic prolixity –'The Committee of Independent Workmen to combat Marxism,' 'The Association for the Promotion of Peace on Working-Class Lines,' 'The German Fighting League for the Breaking of Interest Slavery,' and 'The Political Workers' Circle'. One such group, 'The German Workers' Party', was the subject of an investigation by the *Reichswehr* political department, and Hitler was the man ordered to investigate it.

At one of the Party's meetings he met its founder, Anton Drexler, its Chairman, Karl Harrer, and two of its members, Captain Ernst Röhm and Dietrich Eckart. Drexler was a railway worker of little intelligence and less ability; Harrer was a 'penny-a-liner' newspaper man; Röhm was a brutal homosexual on the staff of the Reichswehr's Munich Command and Eckart was an alcoholic mendicant who dabbled in poetry and drama. These men gave the German Workers' Party – all told there were fewer than fifty members – such driving force as it had.

It was a makeshift organisation that Hitler at once recognised as being ready for knocking into shape under his own leadership. Its aims were ill-definedly nationalistic, anti-Republican, pro-Aryan. Such aims were general among the numerous splinter groups; but only Drexler's German Workers' Party was in that malleable state ripe for vigorous leadership. Hitler saw at once that he could start within it the political career on which he was determined. Within a few months he had become its chief of propaganda and on 1st April 1920 addressed a meeting of 2,000 people in the Munich *Hofbräuhaus* in which he presented the tenets of the newly named 'National Socialist German Workers' Party'– *Nationalsozialistische Deutsche Arbeiterpartei*, from the first word of which the abbreviation 'Nazi' sprang.

Hitler had two great gifts. One was his brilliance as a military tactician, the other was his faultless insight into the psychology of the masses. This ability enabled him to see at once that, as William Shirer says, 'what the masses needed were not only ideas – a few simple ideas, that is, that he could ceaselessly hammer through their skulls – but symbols that would win their faith, pageantry and colour that would arouse them, and acts of violence and terror, which, if successful would attract adherents (were not most Germans drawn to the strong?)

and give them a sense of power over the weak.'

The pageantry, colour and symbols were to come with the adoption of the swastika in the Nazi flag and the stirring rallies to be held at Nuremberg and elsewhere. The perpetrators of the acts of violence and terror were already at hand. They were for the most part beefy roughnecks, unemployed ex-servicemen and sometime convicts to whom the Party paid a few pfennigs for attendance as 'bouncers' at political meetings. Organised into *Ordnertruppen* and commanded by an ex-burglar called Emil Maurice, they escaped suppression under Article 177 of the Versailles Treaty, which forbade the formation of para-military organisations, by calling themselves the Party's 'Gym-

Left: The Nazi party's exploitation of theatrical spectacle reaches its peak in the rallies of the 1930s. *Below:* In 1921 the Brownshirts were confident enough to drop the euphemism 'Gymnastic and Sports Division', and emerged as the *Sturmabteilung* (SA), the Storm Troops

nastic and Sports Division'. But by the end of 1921 they had boldly adopted the name 'Storm Troopers' (*Sturmabteilung*, abbreviated to SA) and were being secretly armed from the armouries of the *Reichswehr*. And they had extended their duties from throwing out hecklers at Hitler's meetings to smashing up the meetings of rival parties. In their brown shirts and jackboots, wielding clubs and supported by machine-guns, they surrounded the halls where Hitler was to speak and by threat or actual violence kept silent the opponents who had infiltrated from, particularly, the Communist underground.

Thus the Bavarian political scene was already subjected to a dominating Nazi influence of terrorism when Himmler arrived almost unintentionally in its midst in 1921. He was then still a student at Munich University. His studies in agriculture included plant biology, soil fertilisation, and chemistry, and all of them were to have a significant effect on his professional life as a genocidal exterminator as well as on his finicky obsession with his own health.

That concern, which had manifested itself in abortive attempts to prove himself physically tough, sporty, and game for anything, but had resulted only in a small but coveted duelling scar, had gained him a certain amount of tolerant affection. His efforts in the students' gymnasium were ludicrously feeble – he couldn't even hoist himself onto the parallel bars – but he gave the impression of being wryly self-deprecatory, of talking contemptuously of his lack of prowess before others got in below his guard.

Cast in an unheroic mould, Himmler turned naturally to the contemplation of heroes – both real and symbolic – and metaphorically fell at their feet. His symbolic 'heroes' included the founder of the Nordic-Indo-Germanic race, a curiously elusive father-figure very properly invisible in the vapours of heredity; the legendary Siegfried was another. Walter Darré, a nonentity born in South America and educated in suburban London, author of a crackpot Nazi testament called *Blood and Soil*, which emphasised the essential nobility of Nordic peasants and the poisonous infiltration into the holy Aryan bloodstream of Slavonic and Jewish ichor, later became another; Ernst Röhm, with his pig eyes and thick neck, and Adolf Hitler, despotic maniac, unsurprisingly were main entries in the Himmler Book of Heroes.

Of these last, Röhm was the first to cross Himmler's path. They met for

the first time on 26th January 1922 at a session of the Munich students' duelling and shooting section. Röhm was ostensibly an instructor there; but his main purpose was twofold: to find homosexual partners and to spread the doctrine of the newly founded Nazi Party, for whose meetings he had supplied some of the SA thugs to 'keep order'. A secondary purpose was to seek candidates for the SA and arm them with weapons and ammunition smuggled out of the armoury of the Munich garrison. Himmler noted in his diary that he was 'extremely friendly' at first, then revealed 'great intellectual strength about the threat of Bolshevism'.

The friendliness was doubtless homosexual exploration which predictably waned on discovering Himmler's unresponsive nature; the 'intellectual strength' could have been no more than the cunning of a political hanger-on who detected a nidus where he might broadcast the seeds of his enthusiasm of the moment. Evidently he was successful, for Himmler was soon enrolled as a member of the *Reichskriegsflagge*, another of the innumerable para-military *Freikorps* formations which, in the complex and unstable situation of postwar Germany, sprang up throughout the country and were tolerated not only by the Weimar Republic, but even by the Allied Control Commission, because they were needed to put down the continual revolutionary threats of other illegally armed groups. Men

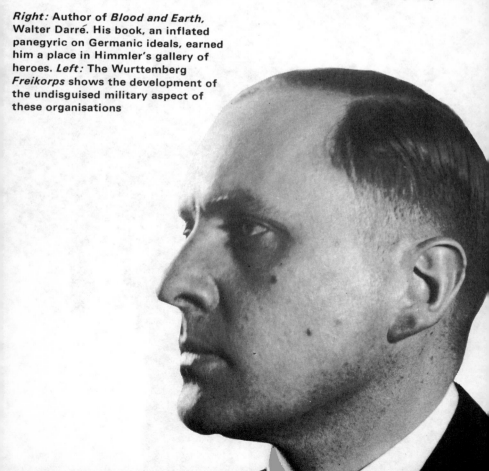

Right: Author of *Blood and Earth*, Walter Darré. His book, an inflated panegyric on Germanic ideals, earned him a place in Himmler's gallery of heroes. *Left:* The Wurttemberg *Freikorps* shows the development of the undisguised military aspect of these organisations

like Röhm latched upon these farcical circumstances as an opportunity to start their own contingents of the *Freikorps* so that whichever way the wind blew they would be sure of some kind of power.

From the *Reichskriegsflagge* Himmler applied for membership of the Nazi Party in the summer of 1923. He had by that time graduated from Munich University with a degree in agriculture and had become a salesman of chemical fertilisers at the firm of Stickstoff, whose factory was at Schleissheim, a few miles north of

Discussions take place at the War College during Hitler's trial. During his incarceration Himmler worked gratis for Röhm

Munich. His membership of the party was probably no more than a youthful enthusiasm inspired by Röhm. Evidently his parents approved because we find him noting, 'My dear father and mother told me that it was their heartfelt wish to see Prince Rupprecht once more on the throne of Bavaria and that I need have no reserve about supporting Herr Hitler in his aim in this direction.'

Herr Hitler's aim was very far from the restoration of any monarch, but the name of the Pretender to the throne of Bavaria was politically useful to him, and his henchman Röhm used it freely as an inducement when setting forth the aims of the Party to political ignoramuses such as Himmler.

Thus we find the so far non-political fertiliser salesman enlisting in the ranks of the Nazis for no better reason than a vague belief that he was exploiting the greatness of Germany's nationalistic heritage – a big drum that Hitler boredly beat whenever the opportunity occurred – and restoring a minor figure of the Bavarian court, which had included, until he was killed in action in 1917, his Godfather and namesake, Prince Heinrich. There is no evidence that at this time he had come directly under Hitler's influence or even that he had heard the Führer in any of his endless tirades. Number two in the Himmler Book of Heroes was still, to him as to many others, only a shabby figure on the horizon of history.

Nevertheless, the potential Nazi proselyte was in evidence at the first famous episode in Nazi history – the *Putsch* of 8th and 9th November 1923. Like Sister Anna, he carried the banner – whether because he was ordered to or because he pleaded for some honour cannot now be established. But there he is, in a newspaper photograph of the time, standing behind the Dannert wire barricades, with the standard in the crook of his arm and an earnest expression on his face.

The *Putsch*, of course, ended in ridiculous failure. The story is too well known to need more than brief summary here. The 3,000 SA marched through the Munich streets led by Hitler, Göring and General Ludendorff and were shot at and dispersed by a handful of civil police with a machine gun as they approached the War Ministry building, where Röhm and his *Reichstkriegsflagge* contingent – including Himmler – were in occupation.

Himmler joined one of the numerous *Freikorps*, trained bodies of 'civilians' which were to become the armed forces of the Third Reich

The resulting trial for high treason got Hitler a five-year sentence and proscription of the Nazi Party. For Himmler, who had taken leave without permission from Stickstoffs to take part in the march there was no job to go back to. But in the glow of his enthusiasm at having found a niche in which he fitted, he was untroubled. He directed his energies into the unpaid work that Röhm, busily prosecuting the aims of yet another revolutionary movement with extremely anti-Semitic aims, was able to give him.

It was very minor work – campaigning for members, making rather feeble speeches along the party line, running

Left: Gregor Strasser's evaluation of Heinrich was 'no world-beater'; but Himmler was pleased with the title *Abgeordneter Ortsgruppenleiter* (District Organiser). *Below:* The Strasser brothers, Otto and Gregor, were among those elected to the Reichstag as *Voelkische* party representatives. Otto argues (below left) earnestly at a meeting. Gregor, (below) on Hitler's right against the draped table, concentrates

messages (which he did on his own motorcycle) and finding rooms to rent for offices. The *Völkische* movement was intensely nationalistic (the word means 'pure German') and drew to itself the support that would have gone to the Nazis had they been legally established. Indeed, in the 1924 elections Röhm, Ludendorff and two brothers named Otto and Gregor Strasser were among those elected to the Reichstag as representatives of the *Völkische* Party. At the elections a year later, however, only Gregor Strasser retained his seat. By that time Hitler, having been released from prison after serving only a year of his sentence, set about re-establishing the Nazi Party.

He had little difficulty in doing so, though he was banned from making public speeches because his release was on parole terms. In the event it was a profitless ban, for there were plenty of others to make all the necessary speeches at the Party Rally that was held in Munich on 27th February 1925 – particularly Gregor Strasser, who had an effective platform personality and brilliant organisational ability. He also had considerable independence of spirit and was by no means prepared to accept Hitler as overlord of the Nazis. Nor, for that matter, was Röhm, who saw himself as military dictator of Germany rather than merely the leader of the SA. An easy solution presented itself for him in an offer to go to South America as a colonel in charge of training the Bolivian army – a job in which he saw a great future for himself. His resignation from the Party in April 1925 left Hitler with only Gregor Strasser as a serious rival for leadership.

He turned the threat into an advantage by persuading the Strasser brothers to undertake the job of organising the Nazis in north Germany with their headquarters in Berlin, where resistance was greatest. Otto immediately and successfully started the northern Party newspaper *Berliner Arbeiterzeitung*, while Gregor

tirelessly campaigned for new supporters of the Strasser brand of Nazi doctrine – which was far more inclined to meld with other nationalistic groups and to place less emphasis on Hitler's leadership; a dangerous fact that Hitler noted and planned to deal with in due course, when he expected to be less dependent on the Strassers' aid.

Himmler meanwhile had been given paid work in the revived Nazi Party by the Strassers. This was not surprising. Both families had roots in Landshut, where the Strassers ran a successful pharmacy and had been among Himmler's customers before he had received his congé from Stickstoffs. Gregor Strasser, a broad, booming man of cheery disposition, several years older than Himmler, adopted a fatherly attitude towards his young protégé and gave him minor secretarial duties. 'He's devoted to me,' Gregor said to another Party member, Kurt Lüdecke, 'and he's very ambitious, but I shan't take him along north [to Berlin]. He's no worldbeater, you know.'

Himmler, avid as ever to fetch and carry, a rigid self-disciplinarian and a brilliant organiser of office routines, was perfectly content with his salary of 120 Deutschmarks a month. But he had a weakness for grandiloquent titles, however worthless; and Strasser saw no harm in that. He therefore appointed Himmler his deputy as 'district organiser' of the Party in Lower Bavaria upon his departure for Berlin. To be known as an *Abgeordneter Ortsgruppenleiter* appealed strongly to Himmler. He acquired at the same time, as a corollary of the deputy district leadership of the Party, the position of second-in-command of an inner group of the SA – that small *corps d'élite* of Shock Troops called the *Schutzstaffel* or SS. That position, fortuitously acquired, was not for long to remain one of insignificance. Fate had thrust Himmler into the nucleus of what was to become the Gestapo.

The organisation

**Ambition and obedience to the rules
rewarded; Himmler enthroned**

Of the founding of the SS Hitler is recorded as saying (in *Hitler's Table Talk*): 'Being convinced that there are always circumstances in which élite troops are called for, I created in 1922-23 the "Adolf Hitler Shock Troops". They were made up of men who were ready for revolution and knew that some day things would come to hard knocks. When I came out of Landsberg [the fortress jail in which he served his sentence for the Munich *Putsch*] everything was broken up and scattered in sometimes rival bands. I told myself then that I needed a bodyguard, even a very restricted one, but made up of men who would be enlisted without conditions, even to march against their own brothers, only twenty men to a city (on condition one could count on them absolutely) rather than a dubi-

Hitler leaves the Landsberg Fortress at the end of his gaol sentence. During his imprisonment party organisation suffered from schism, fortunately for Hitler

ous mass, It was Maurice, Schreck, and Heiden who formed in Munich the first group of toughs, and were thus the origin of the SS; but it was with Himmler that the SS became an extraordinary body of men, devoted to an ideal, loyal to death.'

Hitler's *Schutzstaffeln* bodyguard squads amounted to only 167 picked men within the much larger SA which was 70,000 strong when Himmler acquired its deputy leadership as a kind of throwaway that went with the position of Strasser's understudy as Gauleiter of Lower Bavaria. He himself was given the SS number 168 when Strasser posted him to Munich in 1925. The SS chief to whom Himmler was appointed second-in-command was Erhard Heiden, who in turn was subjected to the rule of Emil Maurice, the sometime burglar who still organised the SA.

The SS was not only small in numbers; it entirely lacked the dignity and traditions of a *corps d'élite* in the accepted sense. The subsidiary task of the Munich section – a task organised with diligence by Himmler – seems to have been to collect Party subscriptions and tout for advertising for the Nazi newspaper *Völkischer Beobachter*. Presumably such lowliness was compensated for by an assumption of some mysterious prestige. It certainly had no financial compensations. SS members had to buy their own black tunic and boots (they wore them with SA breeches and caps) and pay SS as well as Nazi Party dues; and their tour of 'protection' duty was continuous when Hitler was in their district.

At what stage after his humble appointment as SS deputy commander Himmler met Hitler it is difficult to establish. He certainly never became a member of the Führer's innermost circle of cronies, which included such men as Göring, Goebbels and Speer But the Führer's influence on Himmler's career was by no means retarded by lack of personal contact. In 1926 he appointed Gregor Strasser as Reich Propaganda Chief (to the bitter cha-

grin of Josef Goebbels, who was given instead the appointment of Gauleiter of Berlin), and in that way yet another minor office fell into Himmler's hands – that of Deputy Propaganda Chief. In all things the piously enthusiastic Munich nonentity seemed to be Strasser's shadow. The splendour of the titles, however, was all he needed to satisfy his simple conceit. Gothic

Above: Emil Maurice, ex-burglar and SA organiser, marches during the ceremonies commemorating the 10th anniversary of the Munich *Putsch*.
Right: Goebbels was an early intimate of the Führer, unlike Himmler. The Gestapo chief's activities did not suffer as a consequence

goldleaf lettering on the doors of both his office and his modest lodgings told all comers that he was 'Deputy Leader of the National Socialist German Workers' Party, District of Munich. Deputy Chief of the Protection Squads of the Führer, Munich Troop. Deputy Head of Propaganda of the German Reich.' His name appeared in subdued lettering: it was not the display of his name that filled him with pleasure but that of his appointments.

Grandiose though those offices were in name, and empty though for the time being they were of meaning, Himmler made of them everything that could possibly be made. He instituted filing systems covering every aspect of his undemanding duties. One finds him writing to Kurt Lüdecke, an

associate of the Strassers' who was almost as violent in his anti-Semitism as the notorious Julius Streicher: 'Dear Herr Lüdecke, Excuse me bothering you with this letter and taking the liberty of addressing a question to you. Perhaps you know that I am now working in the management of the district of Lower Bavaria for the Party. I also help with editing the local "folk" journal the *Kurier für Nieder-Bayern*. For some time I have entertained the project of publishing the names of all Jews, as well as of all Christian friends of the Jews, residing in Lower Bavaria. However, before I take such a step I should like to have your opinion, and find out whether you consider such an undertaking rich in prospects and practicable. I would be very indebted to you if as soon as possible you would give me your view, which for me is authoritative, thanks to your great experience in the Jewish question and your knowledge of the anti-Semitic fight in the whole world.'

Lüdecke replied, wholeheartedly approving the list, and Himmler began its compilation with an efficiency that was to have grim results. He was no less efficient in compiling indexes of significant trivia – for example the musical and philosophical tastes of those Party members with whom he came in social contact: 'Schwarz was playing *Mendelssohn* on his gramophone when I arrived. It is as well to know of Semitic sympathies.' 'Calling today for Heinz Mücke's subscription I noticed in his bookcase a copy of [Houston Stewart] Chamberlain's *Foundations of the 19th Century*. He is well chosen for the Führer's personal troop.'

In eavesdropping he was equally thorough: 'In the fishmonger's there was a man who mentioned in a low voice to his wife that he suspected treachery in the ranks of the Party. I made it my business to find out his name from the shopkeeper. Such information might be useful in the future.'

For four years Himmler was to burrow industriously and silently away at his highly organised acquisition of information. He reported regularly to the jovial Gregor Strasser, accounting conscientiously for his time and asking for no more expenses from Party funds than provided him with even more filing cabinets and card indexes. Strasser treated him with an amused scorn – 'He is very eccentric but utterly reliable' – and laughed heartily when he heard that

Himmler, immersed in his beloved dossiers

Himmler had carefully kept the oddments of personal information on his fellow cadets he had collected during his spell as an orderly-room clerk in the army. 'Whatever use do you suppose will derive from knowing who did fatigue duties for insubordination in the 11th Bavarian Infantry Regiment in 1919?' Himmler replied that 'one never knows' in a crestfallen manner. His brother Ernst later recalled that during his schoolboy enthusiasm for philately Heinrich had amassed thousands of worthless duplicate stamps for just the same reason:

'He thought that even the Bavaria five-pfennig might some day disappear, leaving him with a cornered market.'

It was as well for his ultimate purpose – slowly materialising in the climate of violent anti-Semitism that now had become one of the driving forces of the Nazi Party – that the organization of the SS lay fallow for those four years from 1925 to 1929. He had time not only to build up his

Alfred Rosenberg, racial theorist and editor of the *Voelkischer Beobachter*

library of dossiers but also to study even more intently the racial theories propounded by the pro-German Briton, Houston Stewart Chamberlain, and the equally pro-German Estonian Alfred Rosenberg, editor of the *Völkischer Beobachter*. Both men theorised on the essential 'purity' of the Nordic-Aryan race.

Chamberlain's *Foundations of the 19th Century* had plundered Gobineau's *Essay on the Inequality of Human Races* and Chamberlain in turn was plundered by Rosenberg in *The Myth of the 20th Century*. All of them tediously preached the sermon that races are unequal in quality, that interbreeding therefore weakens the stock of the higher strains, that of all the Aryan races the Nordic-Teutonic is the highest in intellectual and physical achievement, and that Christianity, with its decadent doctrine that all races share an equality of soul, is 'a vicious and insidious illusion'.

For an industrious yes-man with time on his hands and with the encouragement of Hitler's chauvinistic speeches, racial theories made compulsive reading. It was no fanaticism of character that made Himmler follow the racialist line: it was simply his capacity to absorb influences that happened to be around. That capacity compounded easily with anti-Semitism, with which he was already familiar from his student days – and which, indeed, was an essential part of the theory.

'It is essential that the purest blood-stock of the noble Nordic peasantry, whose blood is as rich as the soil whose husbandry is their concern, should breed and multiply until their blond and shining youth outnumbers and destroys the corrupt Slavs and Jews whose blood poisons the bloodstream of the entire human race and who linger in the dark unhealthy streets of towns and cities.'

To the humourless all things are serious, and there is no indication that Himmler ever revealed a spark of humour. All such propaganda turned out by the H S Chamberlain school of quasi-philosophers was grist to be ground in the mill of his assimilative mind.

So, while the fallow years of the SS passed, Himmler paid increasing unrewarded homage to his Führer by slowly and inexorably stuffing his filing cabinets and widening his knowledge of racial theory. Possibly he hoped for recognition if Hitler ever deigned to glance his way; but he was completely unlike so many other Nazis in that he never jostled for power, never seriously schemed for anyone's downfall. His machinations always lay in the direction of slavishness, not power. When, in the fullness of time, more and more power was thrust upon him he did not, according to his own lights, abuse it. (Indeed in one field, that of an army commander, he failed even to use it profitably for the war effort.) Servility was his bane, not megalomania.

During the dormant years of the SS Himmler did very little travelling. But he did go once or twice to Berlin, where Gregor Strasser and, later, Josef Goebbels held sway. He also went to Berchtesgaden, presumably to indulge his masochistic turn for athletic enterprises – skiing in this case. There he met a woman called Margarete Concerzowo. She was seven years older than Himmler and her family had come from Poland. Her profession was nursing and she owned a private clinic for homeopathic treatment in Berlin.

Himmler's first meeting with her, according to Otto Strasser, had all the elements of a piece of romantic fiction. He encountered her in the lobby of the Berchtesgaden hotel and in taking off his Tyrolean hat with an exaggerated flourish spattered her with melting snow that had accumulated in its brim. His flowery contrition charmed her and soon they were conversationally acquainted and he was discussing herbal remedies with her.

At that time the intestinal pains

that were later to affect Himmler's life – and, as we shall see, the lives of others too – had not taken such a grip upon him. But he had spasms at long intervals and the injections of narcotics with which he had been treated had little effect. Margarete told him that at her clinic little respect was paid to the fashionable treatment by the physicians of the day, but that more simple herbal cures and homoeopathic prophylactics were offered.

Margarete was a large, blonde, dominating woman of Nordic type with

Union of Art and Politics State Theatre drama director Hans Johst and Himmler the married man. Seated are Frau Himmler and Frau Edit von Coler, also of the State Theatre

wide hips and big hands. Her interests included mesmerism, astrology, and curative hypnosis, and she was almost fanatical about open-air life. Gerald Reitlinger in his book *The SS: Alibi of a Nation* remarks scoffingly: 'Buried in the Cotswolds, Heinrich Himmler and his Marga could have cultivated their herbs, clothed in homespun wool, and nurtured on wholemeal bread, occasionally throwing peasant pottery or playing duets on reconstructed medieval instruments.'

Typically, there was no rushing into marriage. Himmler returned to Munich and their courtship was continued in frequent letters in which long discussions about remedial exer-

cises and mythical German heroes were interspersed with coy references to Himmler as a 'naughty darling' and Marga as a 'flower of all womanhood'. During 1927 and the early part of 1928 they prodded at each other's characters as if haggling in a street market. The proddings revealed that they were born under the zodiacal signs 'proper' for marital bliss, that they could profit by interdependence, that both were thrifty and excessively efficient, and that both hankered after a domesticated life with all the windows open and the smell of well fertilised herbs drifting in from the garden. This established, Margarete sold her clinic and bought a chicken

farm in a suburb of Munich called Waltrudering.

By June 1928 they had plighted their peculiar troths and Himmler had slipped so far from the path of sexual virtue that he had marked out for himself that Margarete was pregnant by him. In an unburdening that was half guilt, half pride, he told Otto Strasser that he had lost his virginity.

'And about time,' Strasser replied scornfully.

They were married two weeks later. Their marriage certificate describes Himmler as an 'agriculturist and political executive' [*Gewalthaber*] and Margarete as a 'hospital matron' [*Oberin*]. From Waltrudering Himmler

Left: The happy pair. *Above:* Christmas festivities, 1925

commuted daily to Munich on his motorcycle, tirelessly dedicated now not only to the cares of office but also to selling farm produce and, presumably, gazing rapturously at the blonde Frau whose ancestry he had conveniently discovered to be pure 'Indo-Germanic' in spite of the Slav origins of the Polish race. He conscientiously filed details of his genealogical researches into Marga's ancestry in his ever more numerous dossiers. Also, he transferred the gold-leaf sign board from his lodgings to the gate of the farm, where it was paired off with another, equally impressive, reading 'Marga and Heinrich Himmler. Chicken Farming, Agriculture, Husbandry. Fresh eggs always available. Tilling and harvesting machinery for hire. Herb gardens.'

During the next few months the personnel structure of the Nazi Party underwent considerable and sinister changes.

'The depression which spread over the world like a great conflagration towards the end of 1929,' says Shirer, 'gave Adolf Hitler his opportunity, and he made the most of it. Like most great revolutionaries he could thrive only in evil times, at first when the masses were unemployed, hungry and desperate, and later when they were intoxicated by war. Yet in one respect he was unique among history's revolutionaries: he intended to make his revolution *after* achieving political power. There was to be no revolution to gain control of the State. That goal was to be reached by mandate of the voters or by consent of the rulers of the nation – in short, by constitutional means.'

The way first of all had to be cleared, however, and there was a great deal more opposition in the Party than Hitler's single-mindedness would tolerate. He had appointed Goebbels Gauleiter of Berlin because he was 'an impassioned orator, a fanatical nationalist, and a vituperative writer' and could be relied upon to bring to heel the numerous SA roughnecks who had rallied to Gregor Strasser's more moderate Nazism – which, indeed, was inflected by far too much socialism, even Communism, for Hitler's peace of mind.

While Goebbels was going enthusiastically about his work in Berlin (which consisted mainly of rooting out the most dangerous SA men and dismissing them from the Party) Hitler was equally enthusiastically making new appointments in the south. One of these was the replacement of Major Erhard Heiden as chief of the Munich SS by his deputy, Himmler.

This move by Hitler had also been brought about by threats from the SA. One of Röhm's homosexual partners, Edmund Heines, had originally

been given command of the Munich branch of the SA but had been removed by the SA chief Emil Maurice on Hitler's instructions. That was in 1925, just before Röhm resigned from the party to go off to Bolivia. It had in fact been assumed that Röhm's resignation was caused as much by pique over Heines' removal from office as from anything else, and that he would take his lover with him. But evidently there had been some sort of quarrel and Heines had been left in Munich to kick his heels and smoulder vindictively in the lower ranks of the SA to which he had been demoted.

Now, in the latter part of 1928, there was strong pressure on Hitler to have Heines reinstated as SA chief in Munich. It came mainly from General Franz Ritter von Epp, commander of the Munich garrison of the Reichswehr and the principal financial power behind the *Volkischer Beobachter*. But

Dr Goebbels in leathers. The propaganda-minister-to-be zealously pruned the SA of its more dangerously ambitious shoots

General Franz Ritter von Epp. Despite the general's financial control of the *Voelkischer Beobachter* Hitler ignored his strongly expressed desire to have the homosexual Edmund Heines reinstated as chief of the Munich SA

Hitler refused to be bullied by any Reichswehr General – they all represented, for him, the faction that supported the Weimar Republic and its hated 'November Criminals' – and Heines, with his uninviting background of soliciting in lavatories and clubs, was dropped.

Hitler, who was always wily enough to watch the shadows for concealed ambition, decided that Himmler was the right man to instal as his watchdog – almost in a literal sense, for who would come running to him more willingly with news of any attempted plot than the herb-gardener of Waltrudering? Erhard Heiden, who had started Party life as a volunteer from the civil police, had been given the SS rank of Major and had organized the very earliest bodyguard of six for Hitler in

Left: **The fully fledged** *Reichsführer* **—***Schutzstaffeln***, absolute commander of the SS.** *Below:* **Hitler with SA members in the Berlin Chancellory; Heines grips the Führer's hand**

the days before the Munich *Putsch*, drawing the other five from the heftiest SA members, was altogether too unreliable in Hitler's opinion. His reputation in the civil police had been tarnished by a great many rumours of corruption, and Hitler's invitation to him to join the Party for the 'special mission' of creating the bodyguard probably saved him from dismissal. He was therefore cast aside and Himmler was given his command.

A few days later Hitler had second thoughts. According to Himmler in a speech he made to Wehrmacht officers in January 1937 those second thoughts were concerned with the complete reorganization of the SS, not only the Munich branch.

'The Führer saw plainly that at this time in the progress of the Party the *corps d'élite* on which he had set so much store had not had a fair chance to develop,' Himmler records. 'Its potential was great but its expansion was constricted by the overpowering pressure of the SA. Special training was needed; but, far more than that, an unremitting and incorruptible loyalty was essential. I told the Führer that in my view such incorruptible loyalty could only come from a very special strain of men; that I could find those men; and that it was not too much to promise that the future of the Reich would be secured by the inception of such a corps.'

Although Hitler is known to have been irritated by Himmler's more cranky racial notions (rather than amused, as Gregor Strasser was), it is evident from the scrap of *Table Talk* quoted at the beginning of this chapter that he was by no means averse to the idea of reorganisation along the lines Himmler suggested. At all events, on 6th January 1929 Himmler was given an additional appointment. This time it was not parochial but national. He became *Reichsführer-Schutzstaffeln*, absolute commander of the SS throughout Germany.

He had indeed had greatness thrust upon him.

The build-up

Decorative trumpet banner of the
Adolf Hitler SS Division at the 1933
Nuremberg Rally

Himmler was not the man to let the glory of his new command go to his head. In any case, on taking a count he found that there were still fewer than 300 SS men in the whole of Germany; while, as he knew full well, they had no official role other than that of *Ordnertruppen* and were still a somewhat despised splinter group of the SA. But his servile nature was not one to brood resentfully over that. He contentedly set about formulating rules that would raise both the prestige and numbers of the SS and in doing so demonstrate his obedience to the Führer and the validity of his ideas on what the *corps d'élite* should be.

There is a school of thought which, in its determination to give Himmler all the attributes of a genocidal maniac, insists that his inherent absolute evil was in the ascendant from the time of his appointment as Reichsführer SS. But the belief that Himmler began to seek 'the final solution' in 1929 is manifest nonsense. 1929 to 1933 were the years in which the Nazi Party struggled for power. Their footing, in a Europe beset with the economic troubles thrown off by the Wall Street crash of October 1929, was too insecure for much attention to be paid to solving 'the Jewish question'. The Nazi diatribes against 'the inferior race' were of course in full spate at

Wall Street after the October 1929 crash and a few of the casualties. Europe's economies suffered considerably

every public meeting and in the Party newspapers, but the ubiquity of Jews was not at that time seen as a problem with a workable solution.

The problem of building up and training the SS, however, was one that Himmler could readily tackle. He set about it methodically and without haste. The training programme he organised was rigorous and the discipline gradually became more ruthless. It was obvious as early as the end of January that there was to be fanatical emphasis on racial selection. Every SS man on the roll had to produce documentary evidence of his forebears for three generations. 'Only the loyal in blood can be loyal in spirit' was the slogan with which Himmler justified his insidious investigations. Though

The SS on the march. Members suspected of racial impurity or other grave faults were dropped from the SS and given an allowance tied exactly to the number of parades for which they had been detailed

the Gestapo as such was not yet in existence its foreshadowing was evident in those investigations made in the name of 'loyalty'.

It was not difficult to rid the SS of those whose blood had Slav or 'oriental' strains or whose background was otherwise dubious. They were already SA members and SA members they stayed. All that happened was that they handed in their black tunics and were given an allowance meticulously based on the number of SS parades they had been detailed for. In that way they were shuffled out of the ranks of the *élite* and absorbed in the rabble. Himmler was of course aware of potential reprisals from those found to be ineligible for his aristocracy, but he could oppose the threat with a greater one. His filing cabinets and card indexes had paid off.

'He sat day after day crooning over them like a miser with his gold, his claw-like fingers with their dirty nails flicking through the names of those on whom next to spend his malice.' The

picture is a fanciful one conjured up by an excited journalist too much given to clichés. But it is not entirely baseless. (In one detail it is correct: several people who met Himmler have recorded that he had ugly hands and dirty nails.) It is evident that Himmler spent far too much time in his office to please Marga. Many letters from her, carefully filed by Himmler and now in the Federal Archive, reproach him for working too hard and too long. As their dates advance her tone becomes more tart and she refers to 'neglect of your family' (their child, a girl called Gudrun, was born soon after Himmler's appointment as Reichsführer-SS). 'Next time you come home,' she adds, 'do not bring so many files with you.'

It was undoubtedly this neglect of Marga in favour of 'dutiful concerns of State' – as he often called his work – that led to the breakdown of their marriage. He left her more and more to look after the farm while his devotion to the theories of racialism, and its practice in the cold steel of his filing cabinets, gradually closed in on him as an obsession.

He had by this time forged a close acquaintance with Walter Darré and Alfred Rosenberg. With them he worked for months on details of what was eventually to become the monstrous 'Marriage Law' for SS men – the law dedicated to the breeding at stud of the 'ideal man'.

This paragon, to quote Roger Manvell and Heinrich Fraenkel in their book on Himmler; 'was a fair-haired, blue-eyed super-human athlete whose values were derived from a medieval concept of relationship with the cultivation of the earth, a man who despised most developments in modern culture because he had no judgement in such matters, though . . . he might well play accepted music . . . or read

Gudrun Himmler in 1935. Frau Himmler reproached Heinrich with giving too much attention to his files and not enough to his family

Left: The talented and sadistic Reinhard Heydrich in fencing kit. He personified the ideals of Aryan Purity for the Nazi racists. Ironically he was one quarter Jewish. *Below:* Himmler with *Reichsbauernführer* Darre, whose racist ideas matched those of Rosenberg and Himmler. *Bottom:* Heydrich (right) with Canaris, Hitler's Chief of Military Intelligence

accepted books. He was a man who left all political and social judgements to his leaders, and gave them his unquestioning obedience. Though he might well be in private a kindly husband and an indulgent father, he was essentially a destructive man, ready to act on the vilest and most stupid orders that only served to show the prejudice and cruelty of his commanders. This image of the ideal man,

primitive in his outlook and brutal in his behaviour, was the result of the racial intolerance of Rosenberg, Darré and Himmler, whose collective vision was blinded by the same false idea of past glories which bore no relation whatever to historic truth, to the needs of modern society, or to any future social order which might be called civilised.'

Almost as if at a sign from the mythological gods who formed part of Himmler's increasingly crazy notions there came upon his scene in June 1931 a personification of the marvellous Teutonic hero whose pattern the Himmler-Darré-Rosenberg cabal had been so assiduously framing. This was Reinhard Heydrich with whose brief life Himmler was now to be inextricably entangled.

Heydrich was at that time twenty-seven years old. He was tall, slender, broad-shouldered and handsome in an icy way. His eyes were blue, his nose aquiline, his lips thin, his hands – in contrast to Himmler's – shapely and well kept. He dressed elegantly, was an athlete and swordsman of distinction and a great success with women.

His life so far had had something of brilliance about it. He had exceptional musical talent – his father was head of the Conservertoire of music in Halle-on-Saale, Saxony – and Reinhard had prepared for a professional career as a violinist. He turned that aside, however, at the age of eighteen and entered the navy as a cadet. His training ship was the old cruiser *Berlin*, which had been disarmed and anchored at Kiel. The first officer of the *Berlin* was Commander Wilhelm Canaris, of whom a great deal more was to be heard, and off duty the two became firmly linked socially, Heydrich being invited frequently to the Canaris home to play Haydn and Mozart quartets with Canaris's wife and friends.

Canaris, the man who was to become Hitler's Chief of Military Intelligence, was seven years older than Heydrich. His career during the First World War had been notable for espionage and daring escapes through the Allied naval blockade. It was the kind of career that attracted Heydrich very strongly. For the two years in which he served under Canaris he never lost sight of his objective: to become a naval Intelligence officer. By the time he passed from cadet to midshipman, in 1924, and from midshipman to sub-lieutenant and lieutenant in 1926, he had made sure through Canaris that everyone in high places who could help him was furnished with full details of the so far wholly admirable work of *Oberleutnant* Heydrich.

But Heydrich's career was soon to suffer a major reverse. In the summer of 1930 he seduced a girl who became pregnant; at Christmas the same year he became engaged to Lina von Osten, who had recently left Kiel High School. There was a showdown of intensity when the pregnant girl's father, in a table-thumping scene in which a horsewhip was one of the props, demanded that Heydrich should marry his betrayed daughter. Heydrich declined. It was not compatible with the honour of a German naval officer, he said, to forsake his betrothed in favour of a passing fancy – always provided the betrothed was willing to remain betrothed, which Lina von Osten was, though her parents were violently against it.

This rather melodramatic scene led to another in the Berlin office of no less a personage than Vice-Admiral Erich Raeder, of whom the apoplectic father of the pregnant girl was a friend; and also to an encounter between him and von Osten. The result of all these histrionic outbursts was that Heydrich was summoned before a naval court and ordered to marry the girl or be dismissed from the navy. He chose dismissal and married Lina

Above: Vice-Admiral Erich Raeder, brought into the affair of Heydrich's wild-oats sowing by the unfortunate girl's father. Heydrich is dismissed from the navy. *Right:* Frau Heydrich, to whom Reinhard was engaged when the results of his earlier adventure became public, with their son. *Far right:* Heydrich's close friend Friedrich von Eberstein who arranged Himmler's first meeting with Heydrich

on 26th December 1931.

Meanwhile, in an effort to find him a job, Lina had introduced him to the politics of the Nazi Party, of which she was a fervent member, and suggested that he joined the SS, which by now had attracted to Himmler's staff a number of German aristocrats. He had a close friend, Freiherr Friedrich von Eberstein, who had already joined and become Himmler's principal staff officer, and it was through him that the meeting with Himmler was arranged on 14th June 1931 at Waltrudering. Though there was little to show it at the time, the meeting changed the course of history.

Himmler had decided to establish within the SS an Intelligence unit whose purpose would be to spy, eavesdrop, and report on Party members – particularly those in the SA, which by this time he recognised as a formidable threat to the build-up of his cherished *corps d'élite*. He was under the impression that Heydrich had been a naval Intelligence officer during his service (in fact he had been only a Communications and Code officer, but Heydrich did not enlighten him) and after giving him a brief test in the form of an essay on his proposals for running an Intelligence unit, told him that he would be employed immediately to start the *Reich Sicherheitsdienst*, the Security Service. His salary was to be 180 Reichsmarks a month (about £13·50 by 1971 values) – a sum that, surprisingly, defies translation into thirty pieces of silver. By Christmas Day 1931 – the day before his wedding to Lina von Osten – Heydrich had been promoted three times and had become a *Sturmbannführer* – the equivalent SS rank of a major in the regular army.

His essay on the formation of a

security organisation had suggested that he would begin by seeking out and appointing informers – they were to be euphemistically called Information Officers – inside the ranks of the SS and adding their specialised information to the vast number of dossiers already existing in Himmler's filing cabinets. Such information could be identified by colour codes and cross-indexed under a variety of heads. 'Information officers,' he con-

Heydrich as Security Chief in his Munich office

cluded, 'if properly trained, are always on the alert, always listening for what they are told to hear.'

He enthusiastically set about establishing the *Sicherheitsdienst*, or SD office, in Munich (it was at Turkenstrasse 23) as early as August 1931. It was a time of ludicrous spy mania throughout the German political scene. In the midst of an economic debacle and an endless jockeying for power, all parties and their numerous splinter groups were concerned with spying on each other. The weakness of their systems – if they can be

called that – lay in their lack of co-ordination. This resulted in a situation in which individuals followed trails of information only to find that they were in effect spying on themselves. One amateur detective in an anti-Hitler group the Strassers had established in Prague set out as if on a paper chase to find the perpetrator of an anonymous threat to murder Otto Strasser. He found that the 'threat' originated in a memorandum he had himself written to the highways department of his own town urging the authorities to do something about the increasing incidence of death on the streets (*Strasse*) caused by speeding motorists.

Heydrich's methods proved to be rather more efficient, even though he was obsessed with the notion that only the British had an effective spy system and that it should be imitated. He seriously belived that 'Every decent Englishman is in the employment of the Secret Service without any need to be specially sworn in and he considers it his natural duty to report to it, inasmuch as the power of England depends basically on the Secret Service, since the victor is he who is best informed. . . .'

Anyone who could seriously believe in such a notion must be naïve; but the belief is irrelevant. Heydrich had a fiery ambition to emulate Canaris in becoming a grey eminence of Intelligence. Like Himmler, he had the typically Teutonic organisational mind. That, plus the ambition, was enough to ensure that he would attain a high standard of efficiency.

There was another, and more sinister, reason for his success. As Joachim Fest says of him in *The Face of the Third Reich*, Heydrich 'was besmirched by an indelible stain and in a melancholy state of "mortal sin": he had Jewish ancestors'. This he naturally knew; but in the years up to his membership of the Nazi Party it had been a matter of little or no account. He had been baptised into the church of Rome, his parents being fervent Catholics, and indeed, as he afterwards told Himmler, he 'went through the unexciting routines of acolyte, choirboy and regular mass attendance'. He had, so to speak, 'grown out' of his Jewishness and at the Halle Reform-gymnasium and the Kiel training school he had taken part in whatever amount of Jew-baiting was politically fashionable. (There had never been as much in central and Baltic Germany as there was in the south and Austria.) He had not even bothered to tell Lina von Osten until in one of her violent Nazi pep talks during their engage-

ment he had half jokingly referred to his own 'quarter Jewishness'. She was shocked and insisted on knowing the full details. Her love for him might endure the buffetings of a compromised lover and a bastard child, but she was by no means sure that it could cope with a racial heritage of the deepest evil.

The details were not very complex, but they had been so vague in his mind that he had to go to the public records office to determine them. His maternal grandmother, Sarah Mautsch, had been converted from Judaism to Catholicism upon marrying his grandfather, Karl Julins

Himmler acknowledges the salutes of the crowd on Party Day 1934

Heydrich. Their son Bruno, Heydrich's father, was born shortly before Karl Julins' early death from consumption. Sarah then married again, this time a man called Isidore Süss (a blatantly Jewish name) who was registered as a Lutheran. It was not, of course, his step-grandfather's blood that ran in Heydrich's veins. The contamination from his grandmother, Lina admitted after long and serious consideration, was very slight. She would overlook it, but she had doubts as to whether the Party would tolerate it.

Heydrich pointed out that he was not anxious to join the Party anyway. Like the majority of naval officers during the late 1920s he thought Hitler something of an upstart, a parvenu with wild ideas completely at variance with the traditions of the armed forces – even the wretchedly small but still aristocratic navy and army permitted by the Versailles Treaty. Lina pointed out in her turn that he was at the moment a cashiered naval officer without a job and that if he was going through with the marriage he had so tenaciously pursued he would have to join the Party to go after the job that von Eberstein had singled out for him.

Heydrich's chosen exit from the dilemma, which led him to the interview with Himmler at the chicken farm at Waltrudering on 14th June 1931, and to marriage with Lina von Osten on 26th December in the same year, was to lead also to his own death at the hands of British agents eleven years later. Furthermore, his association with the Reichsführer-SS, and the linking of their two characters within the milieu of Nazism, increased a thousandfold the horrors and tragedies suffered by those whom Hitler chose to trample on. Likewise, the enemies within the Party were sought, found and crushed in the machinery that Himmler and Heydrich were soon to create.

With the same coy use of euphemism that had described the Storm Troopers as 'the Gymnastic and Sports division' the SD was now let loose upon the Party as a 'Press and Information Department,' giving the impression that it was part of Dr Goebbels' propaganda organisation – a convenient cover. It was more accurately described years later by the Israeli Attorney-General, Gideon Hausner, at the trial of Adolf Eichmann: 'Very soon it became an internal espionage and detective organisation which did not balk at any means for achieving its purposes. Heydrich, who organised and commanded this service, always contended: "One must know as much as possible about people." For that purpose a Party Intelligence network was set up which included confidential agents (*V-Leute*), ordinary agents (*A-Leute*), informers (*Z-Leute*), casual employees (*H-Leute*), and doubtful informants (*U-Leute*). They were happy to receive any information whatever about economic developments, social life, politics, and, especially, about the private lives of Party members. Heydrich wanted to know every possible detail about the members of the Party and their opponents, everything relating to their character and weaknesses; their hobbies and habits; scandals in which they had been involved; their personal desires and love life; the places they frequented; the expenditures and income of industrial firms, the movement of bank deposits – in brief, every item that might possibly be exploited, in one way or another, against a man or an institution, especially if it might be used as a threat for purposes of blackmail. All this was patiently and thoroughly recorded by, in its later years, about 100,000 regularly employed agents, detectives and informers. Nothing in the most intimate lives of all the leaders of the Reich, and afterwards of the leaders and administrators of the whole of Europe, escaped the vigilance of the SD.'

Similarly, Heydrich must have realised, the facts of his own ancestry would not escape the vigilance of the enemies he could not avoid making by running a department designed solely for probing into private lives and eavesdropping on public converse. He made haste, upon his appointment, to ransack the public records offices where the evidence lay and abstract all the documents relating to Sarah Mautsch's birth and change of faith.

Himmler, of course, was no less vigilant. It is unbelievable that such a fanatical collator of information would have failed to investigate the background of a man he was considering employing as organiser of a ubiquitous spy system. Why, it may be wondered, would the head of an organisation already dedicated to anti-Semitism put into a high executive position a man whose blood was suspect? There was no necessity to appoint anyone immediately; furthermore, he had an alternative candidate for the job, an ex-member of the Bavarian political police. The choice, or the postponement of the choice, were equally his.

The answer lies in Himmler's astuteness in recognising on sight a complex character with an inherent racial weakness that could be turned to advantage. Events indeed prove it. Shortly after engaging Heydrich, Himmler went to Hitler and in the manner of an obsequious slave confessing an error, reported his discovery that Heydrich had Jewish blood inherited on the distaff side. Continuing in the same apologetic tone, he suggested that this was justification for Heydrich's expulsion from the Party and 'possible subsequent action'. It was a shrewd approach. It was sure to arouse Hitler's opposition, since the Führer would see, as clearly as Himmler saw, the latent possibilities for blackmailing Heydrich. His megalomania would not permit him to accept any suggestion from Himmler; he would therefore assume the credit for having spotted Heydrich's vulnerability.

'It was a very satisfactory interview,' Himmler later recorded. 'The Führer said himself that Heydrich was a highly gifted but also very dangerous man, whose gifts the movement had to retain. Such people could still be used so long as they were kept well in hand and for that purpose his non-Aryan origins were extremely useful; for he would be extremely grateful to us that we had kept him and not expelled him and would obey blindly. Exactly my own feelings; but it was important to me that the impetus came from the Führer.'

Those, then, were the circumstances that established Heydrich as the head of the SD, a tiny department within the scarcely larger SS – a wheel within a wheel that itself was still within the enormous wheel of the SA.

The chain of command now once again incorporated Ernst Röhm, who had returned from Bolivia in January 1931 and had been immediately reinstated by Hitler as overall commander of the SA. With a design in view that at the time seemed a complete reversal of his previous policy, Hitler also dragged the scandalous Edmund Heines out of the shadows and promoted him to the leadership of the Berlin section of the SA. Thus Röhm and his lover were together again, potential mischief makers in the capital city, harbouring grudges against Hitler in the stronghold of his enemies, the Strassers.

The design, however, was not so irrational as it seemed. In retrospect it became clear that Hitler preferred to have his enemies concentrated in one place, where they could easily be watched by conspirators. In addition to the suave little *Gauleiter* of Berlin, Josef Goebbels, with his strong-arm methods of tidying up the more hostile elements of the SA, Hitler had, at Himmler's instigation, installed as head of the Berlin section of his SS a man called Kurt Daluege. Daluege was a tall, gangling, stupid man whose

The Jewish stain on Heydrich's family history did not escape Himmler's probing eye

workaday job was at the city refuse dump as engineer in charge of the incinerators – a grim hint of the task he was later to undertake. He was an old enemy of the Strassers, who called him 'Dummi-Dummi', and could not have been more carefully placed as a watchful eye on their radical activities, which were now reinforced by the Röhm-Heines threat.

In Munich, where Himmler and Heydrich had set up joint shop, greater tranquillity prevailed. There were few

overt threats to the Party. It was a time for quietly examining the qualifications of those who knocked upon the door of the Reichsführer-SS. This task Himmler left more and more to Heydrich. He himself was constantly kept busy with his racial theories and by his efforts to widen the scope of his training programme for his *corps d'élite*. Also, it seems, it was a time for establishing with meticulous pedantry the vis-à-vis relationship between his new staff officer and himself. On the ground that discipline must at all costs be preserved in a dynasty of loyalty, he insisted that both Heydrich and Lina should address him always as Herr Reichsführer, never as Herr Himmler. At the same time (according to Lina) he revealed cour-

Röhm (centre) at La Paz railroad station, Bolivia. He returned to Berlin from instructing the Bolivians in modern military matters to be appointed overall commander of the SA

teously, almost sympathetically, that he was well aware of the power he held over his protégé: 'In a few generations your alien blood will be bred out.'

One can imagine the confrontation at which those reassuring, and at the same time covertly threatening words were spoken. Himmler on one side of the perfectly ordered desk at which he customarily sat, his stubby fingers with their dirty nails tapping on the surface; his weak eyes blinking behind the pince-nez. Facing him the elegant, almost aristocratic Reinhard Heydrich with the look of 'a corrupted angel' (as he was once described); the two of them assessing the precise degree of power each could bring to bear on the other. Himmler probably thinking that there was nothing that

the grip of blackmail could not twist from Heydrich through his flawed blood; and Heydrich probably recognising that Himmler's growing obsession with racial theories was at the same time a strength and a weakness – a weakness that could be played upon to great advantage.

So it proved. Heydrich developed from that moment a bitter anti-Semitism. Unlike Himmler's, which was, so to speak, merely functional and derived from his probings into

Kurt Daluege, head of the Berlin SA, with Goebbels. Daluege's job as engineer in charge of the city refuse incinerators fitted him for his later employment connected with the concentration camp Jews

German mythology and medieval history, Heydrich's appears to have been based on a masochistic hatred of his own Jewish strain. He refused, of course, to acknowledge that strain once he began his operations in the SD. Various accusations of Semitic origins were in due course to be made against him by enemies within and without the Party and he was to answer them all with libel actions which, as head of the SD, he naturally won. But there is no doubt that, as his biographer, Charles Wighton, says, 'Power was Heydrich's deity' and that he saw clearly that his way to it was by Himmler's anti-Semitic road.

That road was now given a signpost. Himmler's obsessional procuring of evidence that only the great Indo-Germanic-Aryan tribes were fit to

Exterior and interior of the 'Race and Settlement Office', where all questions of blood purity were decided

inherit the earth had been assiduously aided by those fanatics, Alfred Rosenberg and Walter Darré. Darré had been taken on to Himmler's SS staff to organise a department of 'race relations'. This Race and Settlement Office (*Rasse und Siedlungshauptampt*, abbreviated to RUSHA) 'was set up to determine the racial standards required of good German stock, to conduct research into the surviving ethnic groups in Europe that could be claimed as German, and to decide all matters connected with the descent of individuals at home and abroad about whom there were any racial doubts.'

On 1st January 1932 the RUSHA published *The Marriage Law of the Reichsführer-SS*. This was what Himmler and his collaborators in eugenics had formulated from their probings into Nietzschean philosophy. To them it was the first step towards 'the improvement of the human race' – a task they had despotically arrogated

to themselves. In a preamble, the Marriage Law set forth in highflown language the ideals it sought to establish within the SS. It invoked the mysterious 'father figure' from whose loins the great Aryan races were supposed to have sprung; the Nordic hero, Siegfried, with his reforged sword symbolising the conquest of the powers of darkness; and of course the Dark Age and medieval kings of Franconia, Saxony, Bavaria and Swabia who had fought back the Hungarians and Northmen and consolidated the kingdoms. (One of them, Heinrich the Fowler, was claimed by Himmler to be his direct ancestor.) Then it went on to grimly practical matters: 'Each enlisted member of the *Schutzstaffeln*, present and future, is

to make application for, and be issued with, a certificate of approval before marriage.

'His intended bride, her parents and forebears back to the year 1750, will be the subject of the investigations of the Race and Settlement Office, and in the event of evidence of Slav or Semitic blood being discovered the onus of proof to the contrary lies with the accused.

'Evidence of freedom from physical and mental disease and of the ability to bear children must be furnished and will be checked in examination by approved SS doctors.

'The Race and Settlement Office will maintain the Clan Book of the SS in which records of all children of the marriage will be kept.

'The arrangement of the details of marriage petitions is the task of the Race and Settlement Office.

'SS members who in spite of being denied marriage certificates marry nevertheless, will be expelled from the SS.

'By command of the Reichsführer-SS. Heil Hitler!'

Just over a year later, on 30th January 1933, President Hindenburg handed over the Chancellorship of the German Reich to Adolf Hitler. The Führer had achieved his object, as he had always intended, by constitutional means. The future development of the Nazi Party and the German nation was to be along somewhat less constitutional lines. And to add to the impetus behind the Reich the SS soon numbered 30,000.

'The increase,' Eberstein said in his evidence at the Nuremberg trial, 'can be explained first by the fact that the National Socialist government had come to power and a large number of people wanted to show their loyalty to the new State. Also, a great number of aristocrats and members of German princely houses joined and attracted by their distinction. There was Prince von Waldeck, Prince von Mecklenburg, Prince Lippe-Biesterfeld, General Graf von Schulenburg, Prince Hohenzollern-Sigmaringen, and the Archbishops of Freiburg and Brunswick. And the elegant black and silver uniform added to the prestige. It was not difficult to attract members.'

Far left: Berlin's citizens greet the new Chancellor as his car negotiates the jubilant crowds; 30th January 1933. *Left:* Prince Waldeck and other aristocrats attracted many new members to the SS organisation by their own readiness to join

The organisation in action

Himmler as orator

No sooner had Hitler been appointed Chancellor on the afternoon of Monday 30th January 1933 than the thudding footfalls of the SA were to be heard as they assembled in the parks and zoological gardens of Berlin for the triumphal march through the Brandenburg Gate and down Wilhelmstrasse. Their ready presence proves that a Nazi victory had been anticipated, though whether that victory was to be thrust into Hitler's hands or would have to be wrested from the failing grip of the Weimar Republic was uncertain. There had been immense crowds of workers in the pleasure gardens only two days previously, ready to march or strike, they said, if Hitler was made Chancellor. Their mood of hostility had been inflamed by Leftist agitators and sureptitious propaganda by the Strasser faction, which still pressed for a more middle-of-the-road policy than Hitler was prepared to accept. In the event, however, there had been no *coup*, no trouble. Hitler had prepared his ground too well. Secret conferences with ex-Chancellor Franz von Papen, and with President Hindenburg's son and his State Secretary had determined the issue. The opposition of the senile President – he was eighty-six – simply crumbled in the hands of the cabal. Hitler had arrived.

Within a month he had inveigled

Confident SA assemble outside the Communist Party HQ in Berlin, a few days before Hitler's victory

Hindenburg into suppressing all civil liberties by decree 'as a defensive measure against Communist acts of violence endangering the State'. The decree specifically stated that the right of free expression by speech or in the press was restricted; that assemblies in public places were forbidden without permission; that invasion of privacy in postal and telegraphic communication was permitted 'by authorised officers'; and that warrants could be freely issued for the searching of premises and the confiscation of property.

The implication of the decree was that Communist power had become such a threat to freedom that it had to be throttled by its own methods. Hitler's reasoning was sound. Coming from the bourgeoisie himself, he was reasonably sure that the psychological reaction to the decree would be to vote heavily in favour of the Nazi Party at the elections in March.

He was right. 'Millions of the middle class and the peasantry [were thrown] into a frenzy of fear that unless they voted for national socialism at the elections. . . the Bolsheviks might take over,' says Shirer. 17,250,000 of them to be more or less exact. But these amounted to less than half the electorate; so Hitler missed the two thirds majority he needed 'to carry out a new bold plan to establish his

Goebbels, well supported, speaks at the Berlin Sports Arena before the March elections

dictatorship by consent of parliament.' He had no need to worry, though. The absolute power of the dictator was not to elude him for long.

On 21st March parliament formally reassembled. The ceremony gave Dr Goebbels his first big chance as Nazi Minister of Propaganda, to which bishopric of psychological power he had been translated a week after the elections. The Reichstag building having been conveniently gutted by fire three weeks previously (a Bolshevik plot of course), Goebbels set his stage in the most sanctified spot in Germany – the Brandenburg town of Potsdam, where the bones of Frederick the Great are entombed in the garrison church. Not only the setting but also the cast of characters was chosen

to make greatest psychological impact. Prussian military glory was given its head. Every ancient general and admiral who had any link with Bismarck's Second Reich was called from club, military academy, rest home and cemetery gate to come and pay homage to Hitler's Third Reich. Shakos of the Death's Head Hussars, cordons of the Order of the Black Eagle, swastikas, spiked helmets, field-grey uniforms, glittering jackboots, and field-marshals' batons were everywhere evident among the civilian notables. The clicking of heels and the rattling of sabres was evident too. And in the midst of the carefully

Election posters are counted into batches for distribution

staged scene President von Hindenburg and Chancellor Hitler faced each other seated on thrones – the President in his voluminous field-marshal's greatcoat, the Chancellor in formal morning dress (in which he looked clownishly ridiculous).

There was an exchange of speeches in which Hindenburg invoked the spirit of Kaiser Wilhelm by saluting the empty Imperial box in the gallery of the church and Hitler thanked him for handing over the reins of power. Both invocation and gratitude were of course wrapped up in many emptily noble phrases ('May God liberate us from selfishness and party strife' was, perhaps, the emptiest) but the complete transfer of power was what they concealed.

Two days later, the first meeting of the Reichstag was convened. Goebbels had done all he could to furnish melodramatic scenery at the assembly; now he trumpeted the claims of 6,000,000 unemployed to the votes of parliament. 'Only the Nazi Party can cure the evil that has set in,' he said in his newspaper *Der Angriff*. 'The Reichstag *must* vote for the Enabling Act to establish the only law that can remove the distress of the people.'

The Enabling Act was simply the constitutional imprimatur for the power Hindenburg had verbally handed over to the Führer in the garrison church at Potsdam. It gave complete powers of legislation to Hitler's cabinet for a period of four years. He could do virtually anything – including deviating from or overriding the constitution of the nation. The Act was passed by a huge majority – 441 to eighty-four – and by its passage legally established Adolf Hitler as Dictator of Germany. Only the President, whose powers were

Goebbels's set piece in Potsdam. Hindenburg and First World War military chiefs are greeted emotionally by Hitler, Göring, Goebbels and other notables of the new regime

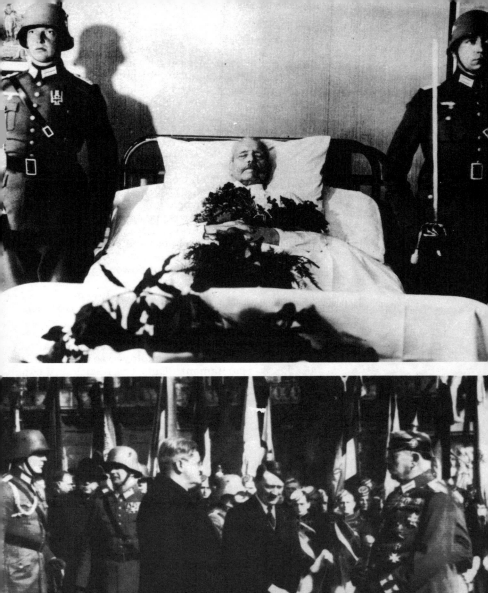

Above: The *Reichsführer-SS* acquired teeth after Hitler's seizure of power. *Above left:* The late Head of State. Well before his death Hindenburg's function was reduced to automatic approval of Hitler's proposals. *Below:* Secretary of State Dr Meissner, Hitler and Hindenburg at a war memorial ceremony

referred to in an aside in the Act's five clauses as 'remaining undisturbed', could in theory veto any legislation of the Nazi cabinet. But Hindenburg had already delegated his powers through his son to von Papen and the State Secretary; he had none left to disturb; the cabal had wrested everything from him save his martial dignity, his spiked helmet, his sabre, his baton and his ribbon of the Black Eagle. He remained in office as President of the dying Weimar Republic for sixteen more months, until, on 2nd August 1934, he too died. The only purpose he served after the Enabling Act was passed was as a rubber stamp of the word 'Approved'.

Hitler's skill in manipulating constitutional forces to his own advantage now became apparent. He had been patient and had made no unguarded moves. Unlimited power was his to command and misuse. The Social Democrats had been his only opponents in the vote for the Enabling Act. Their leaders were swiftly spirited away into 'protective custody' along with the Communists and bandwagon Leftists while their organisations collapsed or were suspended by decree. No official opposition now existed. The trade unionists, who had threatened to strike if Hitler became Chancellor, were encouraged by their own head, Dr Robert Ley, into believing that their unions were 'sacred institutions' which would accordingly be given full protection of their rights. Whereupon, having accepted Ley's assurance and switched their allegiance to Hitler, they were sold down the river by Ley, who treacherously helped the Führer to confiscate the funds, arrest the leaders and occupy the premises of the whole trade union movement. In its stead there was established something called the German Labour Front, which agreed 'to restore absolute leadership to the national leaders of industry, the employers' – and through the employers, of course, to Hitler. Thus the last vestige of power, the power to withhold labour was torn from the people.

Immediately after Hindenburg's death, Hitler's cabinet passed a law combining the offices of President and Chancellor. Since the President was nominal head of all the armed forces, Hitler thus arrogated to himself the fealty of every member of every military and paramilitary organisation in Germany.

The fealty of the fanatically slavish Himmler had never been in doubt. Satisfied with his high-toned titles and his freedom to gather and classify evidence of other people's wavering allegiance, he had willingly remained in the background of Party activities, acquisitive as a magpie, undistinguished as a sparrow. Warmed by the idealistic anti-Semitism of Gobineau, Wagner, H S Chamberlain and Walter Darré, his blood coursed thinly under his pallid skin. He was increasingly subject to colic spasms which he treated – ineffectively – with Marga's herbal tisanes; but he never allowed them to prevent his attendance at his office 'on dutiful concerns of state'. And now with the seizure of complete power by Hitler came the transformation of the Reichsführer-SS from a magpie-cum-sparrow into a hawk waiting to swoop.

Similarly, Reinhard Heydrich had been quietly but assiduously pursuing his activities as an ostensible disciple of Flavius Josephus, the Palestinian Jew who in the first century AD fought against the Roman occupation then betrayed his race for the Governorship of Galilee and the opportunity of committing scientific or merely brutal atrocities upon his fellow Jews. It would be satisfying to know that Heydrich had studied Josephus's *The Jewish War* and to be able to infer that he had found justification for his treachery in that horrifying essay in betrayal. There is no evidence that he did so; all the same, his masochistic hatred and denial of his Jewish blood had spurred him to the accumulation of some 33,000 files of docketed information on Jews in Bavaria alone. It was graded according to reliability; but as he remarked to Himmler, 'Reliability is adjustable.'

Whether conscious or not, Hitler's timing can now be seen to be as accurate as his manipulation of the constitutional forces he had so patiently twisted to his own ends. At the very moment of his achievement of power he had ready all the apparatus necessary to press it home. He was not to fail in his attack because of a breakdown in his lines of communication. He could by no means have foreseen the path of his progress from propagandist in Anton Drexler's shambles of a party to founder of the Third Reich; yet at the beginning of 1929 he had infallibly latched upon Himmler as the watchdog to replace the corrupt Erhard Heiden as Reichsführer-SS. It had been, on the face of things, little more than a grace-and-favour appointment, yet it now proved to be the appointment that had provided everything necessary for the spiriting away of active opponents and the ruthless policing of every corner of the Reich.

In the matters of 'spiriting away' and policing, Himmler's and Heydrich's dedication to their objectives had been extremely fruitful. Hermann Göring, whom Hitler had appointed Minister of the Interior for Prussia in the new administration, had inaugurated the Third Reich's first concentration camps in that State immediately after the suppression of civil

Above: Göring, as Minister of the Interior for Prussia, was the originator of the first concentration camps; Himmler enlarged on the idea, opening the 'experimental' camp at Dachau. *Above right:* Dachau concentration camp from the outside. *Below right:* Inmates at Dachau

liberties at the end of February 1933. But it was Himmler who as President of the Munich Police (another title that had brushed off on him) signed an order on 21st March blandly announcing the opening, the following day, of an 'experimental' concentration camp at Dachau to accommodate 5,000 prisoners.

The Reichsführer-SS, it appeared, was concerned to have camps that were as orderly as his desk and his mind. The ebullient Göring thought of the object, not the method of achiev-ing it. Himmler held the view that 'protective custody' meant precisely that. The State must be protected from the activities of 'racial traitors and Bolshevik agitators' who, singly or collectively, were irritant grains of sand in the machinery of state.

The order for the arrest of suspects was bleakly efficient:

'Based on Article I of the Decree of the Reich President for the Protection of People and State of 28th February 1933 you are taken into protective custody in the interest of public

security and order. Reason: suspicion of activities inimical to the State.'

Those two sentences were to become the formula of terror throughout the Reich. They followed the thunderous knocking on the door at midnight, the pressure of the pistol in the ribs from the adjacent cinema seat, the word 'Gestapo' muttered in the ear by a low voice in market square or public transport. But they were to the Reichsführer-SS no more than the legal means of achieving an arrest. Unlike Göring, however, he could not be satisfied with imprisonment of suspects as an end in itself.

'A great deal of potentially useful information can be extracted from suspects,' he declared in an SS order of April 1933. 'Even if suspicion of their

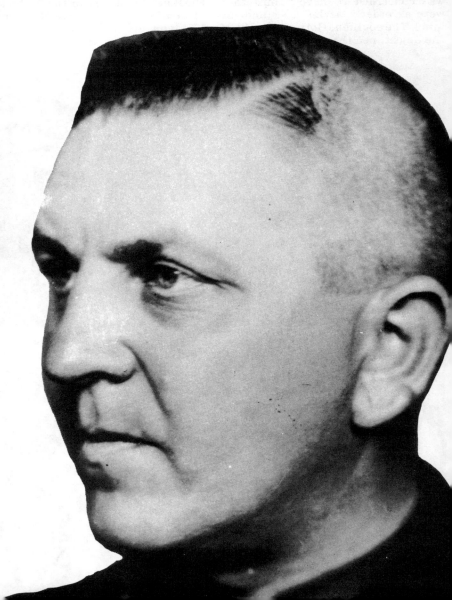

treasonable activities proves to be unfounded they can often be persuaded to give the SD information that will lead to other suspects. Such information is usually readily given under duress, threat, or promise of release.'

The names of some of his henchmen at Dachau sound echoes of horror down the corridors of infamy: Theodore Eicke, Karl Adolf Eichmann, Rudolf Höss. They were given carte blanche for their tortuous designs in the 'Rules for apprehension and concentration' worked out with loving care by Himmler and Eicke (who had been appointed Commandant of Dachau). For example, here are Rules 11 and 12: 'Offenders considered to be agitators are those who make inciting speeches, hold meetings, form cliques, loiter in

Left: Commandant of Dachau, Theodor Eicke. **Below:** Karl Adolf Eichmann of Dachau

Left: 'Offenders ... to be shot or hanged.' '... floggings or other inducements [to implicate others] may first be administered at the discretion of the camp commandant. Extract from Rule 11. The rules were formulated by Eicke and Himmler.
Below: Himmler's therapist Felix Kersten

public spaces; who supply the propaganda of the opposition with atrocity stories, true or false, about the concentration camps, or who receive such information, bury it, talk about it to others or smuggle it out of the camp into the hands of foreign visitors. These are to be shot or hanged on order of the Reichsführer. Where it is to the advantage of the SD – that is, when names of other offenders can thereby be obtained – floggings or other inducements may first be administered at the discretion of the camp Commandant.

'The following offenders, whose crime is mutiny, will be shot on the spot or later hanged: anyone making a physical attack on an SS guard, refusing to obey orders to work, or inciting or making speeches while marching to work. Two weeks' solitary confinement and twenty-five lashes will be awarded to anyone making deprecatory comments in letters or other documents about Nazi leaders, the State, or the Government, or glorifying Bolshevik or Liberal leaders of the old democratic parties.'

One recalls with revulsion Gebhard Himmler's assurance that his brother as a youth was 'kind to old ladies and often ran errands for them and carried their shopping'. There are also many recorded instances of his sentimentalising of the beauty of nature and the wickedness of hunting. Felix Kersten, the therapist who in 1940 was to become Himmler's doctor, quotes his patient as saying 'in an agitated outburst:'

'How can you find pleasure, Herr Kersten, in shooting from behind cover at poor creatures browsing on the edge of a wood – innocent, defenceless, unsuspecting? It is really pure murder. Nature is so marvellously beautiful and every animal has a right to live. It is this point of view that I admire so much in our forefathers. They, for instance, formally declared war on rats and mice, which were required to stop their depredations and leave a fixed area within a definite time limit, before a war of annihilation was begun against them. You will find this respect for animals in all Indo-Germanic peoples.'

Himmler had long been fanatical enough about his racial theories to find support for them in almost anything. For ourselves, there is in the 'agitated outburst' a bright illumination of the dichotomy of Himmler's character. Clearly he seriously believed that if depredatory rats and mice were given an order to clear out within a definite time, the warning being backed by a threat of extermination, the problem of their depredations would be solved without any need for unpleasantness. He was incapable of grasping that rules for any sort of conduct might not be slotted into other minds with the ease with which his own received and cherished them. He saw no anomaly

Early pictures show the comparatively generous treatment of prisoners in Dachau before the war

at all in regimenting all forms of life into accepting the ideals of an all-powerful being – personified in his case, of course, by Adolf Hitler – and was continually puzzled, as he told Kersten, 'that people cannot see the wisdom of conforming to plans made for them by those whose work in life it is to make plans. How foolish it is for them to choose deliberately unpleasantness and even death. Also unpleasant for me. But then it is the curse of the great to have to walk over corpses.'

In this curiously lofty manner he detached himself from the infamous activities that went on in Dachau and its counterparts. Like a lodestone he attracted to himself those who saw in him the channel along which they could pursue the heinous achievement of their perversions. His detachment sprang from his complete inability to equate theory and practice. His henchmen were all crudely realistic in their attitude to life – which to them was synonymous with evil – while for him, Himmler, everything was theory,

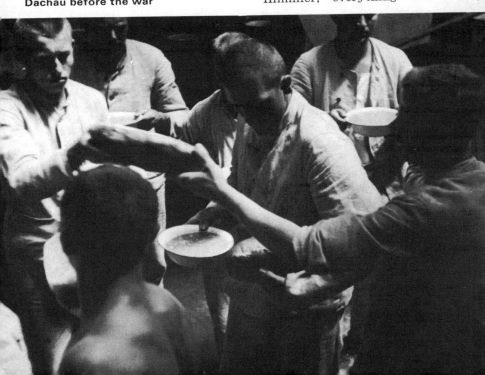

files, the distillation of lives into index cards, the mad assumption that all who fell outside the pale of his racial concepts would scurry away or be annihilated under the law. 'In the last analysis it was this stupendous lack of realism which determined the man's life and character,' says Joachim Fest.

Like the rats and mice of Himmler's idealised 'forefathers', the Indo-Germanic peoples, there were of course hundreds of thousands of Jews who slid silently away from Germany in search of refuge during the early years of Nazi persecution. Some found it; but these were for the most part individuals with international claims to fame – Otto Klemperer, Georg Grosz, Max Reinhardt for example. Those evacuated in shiploads under the compassionate but inefficient wings of philanthropic organisations were usually defeated by the apathy and hypocrisy of the United States and Britain. Although Roosevelt, Cordell Hull, Sumner Welles and a great many other statesmen were continually prodded with informative reports of German plans for the complete elimination of the Jewish race, they appeared to have remained indifferent. There were innumerable conferences to discuss the immigration of fleeing Jews into Britain and America, but they all faded out on such questions as, who should pay the transportation costs? were Jews worthy of any special consideration? what were the true immigration policies of the countries concerned? The shuffling of responsibility from one government to another continued with agonizing caution while the refugees sailed statelessly from port to port.

During the industrious hours when Himmler was a mere cipher in the Nazi movement he had formulated and filed away a 'five-point plan to diminish the influence of Judaism for the protection of German blood and honour'. The plan laid down, specifically, that German citizenship should exclude all Jews; that marriages between Jews and Germans were forbidden; that extramarital relations between Jews and

Anti-Jewish pamphlets distributed in Berlin

Germans were forbidden; that Jews were forbidden to employ German citizens under the age of forty-five as servants; and that Jews were forbidden to show or touch the national flag.

As has been said, such a plan could have been, at its inception, in no way an attempt to put forward 'the final solution'. (The phrase, incidentally, did not come into use until the autumn of 1941.) 'The Jewish problem' had not yet been propounded as such. Himmler's tireless mind was simply mulling over ideas. But this particular idea was nurtured in fertile soil. By 1935 it had reached the status of law and was dressed in legal phraseology by a lawyer called Franz Stuckart. The plan was promulgated and ratified at the Nuremberg rally on 15th September that year. This 'most murderous legislative instrument known to European history' (as Reitlinger calls it) quickly became known as The Nuremberg Laws.

It was of course the first point of the plan, the Reich Law of Citizenship,

that was the most cruel. No Jew could now have recourse to any kind of protection against persecution. They stood outside the State except as subjects of derision and legalised terror, which from then on was unrelenting. And for the purpose of deriding and terrorising no organisation could have been more convenient or more effective than Himmler's SS and Gestapo.

The Gestapo, as such, was a development of the Berlin Police Bureau IA, the political branch of the civil police – who in their entirety came under Hermann Göring's control as soon as he was appointed Minister of the Interior. To Göring, Bureau IA appeared as a potential weapon to combat the power of SA, which since the restoration of Röhm had become far too extensive for Hitler's peace of mind. 'Dummi-Dummi' Daluege was all very well as a lookout for trouble concocted by the Strasser-Röhm-Heines consortium; but his power as head of the Berlin section of the SS was limited – not least by his stupidity and incorrigible vanity, which weakened his guard against every deception practised on him. Göring saw at once that

SS inspection, 1935

Bureau IA was the answer – an undercover force that had powers of arrest and could act on information received from Heydrich's SD. It would, however, need considerable enlargement – a matter not difficult to arrange, and one he put in hand immediately through the Bureau's head Rudolf Diels, who was his own cousin. (Nepotism and corruption went unbridled in Göring's scheme of things.) It also needed a new and more important name, which, in the event, was suggested by a Post Office man. *Geheimes Staatspoleizei* ('Secret State Police'), he pointed out, would abbreviate neatly to Gestapo and fit the franking stamp that would be necessary to authenticate its documents. It was adopted immediately and on 13th June 1933 its constitution was authorised by Hitler who, by that time, was safely guarded by the Enabling Act in any move he cared to make. A force of secret police was something that would prove necessary for various designs he had in mind.

Within six months the Gestapo had effectively extended its powers. As Bureau IA it had been concerned mainly with tracking down and keeping tabs on immigrants whose politics were suspect; now its activities were directed towards Party members and intrigues. Also, in spite of Göring's intentions, both Himmler and Heydrich looked towards its Prussian monopoly: both were concerned to make its activities national rather than regional and their own control absolute.

That turned out to be far simpler than perhaps either of them had expected. One of Heydrich's V-Leute had come up with some information about a Communist plot to assassinate Göring – possibly a genuine plot, though it would in fact have been perfectly simple for Himmler and Heydrich to concoct all the evidence of one. Genuine or not, the plot was not revealed to Göring until the alleged conspirators had been arrested by the SS in Munich. Himmler then cunningly pointed out that some grave fault surely lay at the heart of a secret police organisation that knew nothing of a plot to assassinate its head.

Ernst Röhm and SA leaders

'The fault lies in the regional control system', he wrote in his report to Hitler. 'It is fortunate that the conspiracy originated in Bavaria, where I have control. Otherwise it could have been successful. The remedy, obviously, is to put all the Reich police forces – civil, political and secret – under command of the SS.'

Hitler naturally did not miss the point that by SS Himmler simply meant himself. He was not unaware of Himmler's ambition for titles and control of extensive networks of intrigue. Equally, he was aware of his slavish dedication to the State and all its works. Himmler was not the man to abuse power in any way detrimental to Hitler. On the con-trary, his power, extended, could deal effectively with those like Röhm who were becoming a growing embarrass-ment and threat. It was a risk worth taking.

'As from this date', Hitler ordered in a directive of 1st April 1934, 'all regional Ministries of the Interior will merge with the Reich Ministry of the Interior and all police and security departments, including the Gestapo, will be under command of Reichs-führer-SS Heinrich Himmler, who will be directly responsible through the Reichsmarschall [Hermann Göring] to me.'

With a display of obsequious hand-washing and tearful gratitude Himm-ler declared before the assembled Gestapo on 20th April 1934, 'I shall

forever remain loyal to you, never will you have anything to fear from me.' Continuing along lines of earnest self-sacrifice he told them that, much as it meant to him, he would now give up his farm at Waltrudering and move to Berlin, 'having established my wife and family in a peaceful home at Gmund.' (The family now included an adopted boy named Gerhard.) Having given the Nazi salute he declared again that no-one loyal to the State and the Führer had anything to fear.

Two months later the combined forces of the SS, SD and Gestapo engaged in their first big action under Himmler's direction. This was the famous 'Night of the Long Knives' massacre in which Hitler finally removed the threat of Röhm's enor-mous SA – now at a strength of some 3,000,000 men, using as part of his justification the agreement he had made with Britain's representative, Anthony Eden, who was expressing alarm at Germany's furtive rearma-ment, to demobilise two thirds of the SA and reduce the remainder to an unarmed body more in keeping with its designation as a 'Gymnastic and Sports Division'. 'Only by thus de-ceiving Britain and the other Ver-sailles criminals', he was later to tell the Reichstag, 'could I enable Germany to continue her secret rearmament

A merry trio: Himmler with Göring and Hitler in late 1934. Earlier in the year Himmler was given complete command of the SS, SD and Gestapo

and return to her status as a world power.'

But that was only a segment of the Führer's 'justification'. Röhm and his huge army of brown-shirted Storm Trooper thugs were continually in conflict with the Reichswehr – the regular army (still nominally the 100,000 permitted by the Versailles Treaty), at the head of which stood the Defence Minister, General Werner von Blomberg. Von Blomberg was strongly pro-Nazi; but he and the Army High Command were violently opposed to Röhm and his SA mob: 'Rearmament is too serious and difficult a business to permit the participation of peculators, drunkards and homosexuals.' Since Röhm, who had Cabinet status, was continually urging the amalgamation of the Reichswehr with the SA, SS, and all the so-called

Veterans' contingents, it was clear to von Blomberg that Röhm planned to oust him from the Ministry and himself take command of the entire military and paramilitary forces of the country. An intolerable prospect, as Hitler was firmly warned.

The Führer had to move warily at this stage. He had become Dictator by a series of astute moves and he could be toppled from power without difficulty unless he secured his footing while there was still time. Hindenburg, though dying, was still President and head of all the armed forces and the question of his successor was one of paramount importance to Hitler and the Army High Command. The answer he found was simple. In exchange for the Reichswehr's backing of himself as Hindenburg's successor, the Führer agreed to 'disband, sup-

press, or otherwise neutralise' the SA.

Himmler now stepped into his stride as a disbander, suppressor and neutralizer without rival. The mechanisms of his tentacular organisations moved smoothly into operation. Both he and Heydrich had their most bitter enemies in the SA and the opportunity to be rid of them along with those who at Hitler's command were to be arrested and 'neutralised' was compelling. Nor was justification difficult. Plots, counterplots and subversive activities were as easily uncovered or manufactured as had been the alleged plan to murder Göring that had brought the Gestapo under Himmler's control.

By the end of June 1934 everything was ready for the purge. Heydrich's SD had supplied all the evidence of 'treasonable acts' and fitted the required victims' names to them with considerable skill. The Gestapo had kept track of everyone's movements, the SS firing squads stood by. Hitler flew off from Berlin to Essen on Thursday 28th June to attend a wedding and thereby detach himself geographically from the actions of his chief henchman in the massacre, Himmler.

Throughout that weekend the long knives of murder flashed in the bright sunlight and starry darkness of midsummer. By Sunday the victims had all been slaughtered or imprisoned. Their total number was never known, but there was an official admission on Hitler's part that seventy-seven 'higher SA leaders' were shot or 'died resisting arrest.' In fact there were almost certainly at least 500 and probably nearer 1,000. Apart from

Left: Anthony Eden was alarmed by Germany's accelerating militarism. Hitler killed two birds with one stone by substantially disbanding the 3,000,000-strong SA. This both took care of Röhm and soothed the British representative. *Right:* General Werner von Blomberg had reason to be satisfied at the emasculation of the SA, a rival to his regular army

Above: Dr Dolfuss, Austrian Chancellor. As a prelude to the annexation of Austria his murder by the SS is arranged. *Right:* Himmler and Heydrich in Vienna after the Anschluss. *Below:* SA men and Röhm, centre, before the Night of the Long Knives in which he, Heines and hundreds of others were eliminated

those who opened their doors to hear their visitors utter the new but increasingly familiar word Gestapo and who were then led away to be lined up in front of SS firing squads or be 'interrogated' in the Gestapo headquarters in Prinz Albrechtstrasse, Berlin, there were hundreds who disappeared into the concentration camps, committed suicide or whose mutilated bodies were found in swamps, undergrowth, and empty buildings. The most notable victims included Röhm himself, Gregor Strasser, Edmund Heines and the male lover with whom he was found in bed in a Wiessee Hotel, Karl Ernst (one of those involved in the Reichstag fire plot), General Kurt von Schleicher (Hitler's predecessor as Chancellor), and Gustav von Kahr (sometime President of Bavaria and an old opponent of Hitler).

Just as Hitler had given the signal for the beginning of the massacre by his attendance at a social function, so he closed it by attending another one – a garden party in the Chancellery. Hardly suitable garden party conversation but recorded nonetheless was his comment that 'Everyone must now know for all future time that if he raises his hand to strike the State, then certain death is his lot.'

For Himmler there was the reward of immense satisfaction with the working of his various enterprises; for Heydrich immediate promotion to the rank of Lieutenant-General-SS. For both of them the chance of planning and executing another political murder – that of the Austrian Chancellor, Dr Dolfuss, who was shot by SS men on 25th July. Hitler shed crocodile tears over this event and said he was 'shocked beyond measure'; but it was the first step towards his annexation of Austria, which he was to achieve bloodlessly in 1938. He had every reason to be satisfied with the unspectacular but dutiful efficiency of his Reichsführer-SS and with the terrible apparatus of the Gestapo that he had placed in his hands.

Concentration camps and herb gardens

Chief engineer Max Faust explains the industrial role of Auschwitz to Himmler

In contrast to Hermann Göring, whose extravagances and acquisitiveness cost the State millions, Himmler was obsessively frugal. At no time was he ever interested in money or possessions; and at no time – though he became the most powerful man in Germany next to Hitler – did his salary ever exceed the 1971 equivalent of £1,000 a year. Nor did the slightest breath of financial corruption ever touch him. All totalitarian states are necessarily rife with corruption and racketeering, since everyone has something to conceal, and Hitler's Third Reich was no exception. There was information to be bought and sold, property to be sequestrated, privileges to be exchanged for other privileges, advancement in civil or military organisations to be had for cash, funds to be plundered, judges to be bribed.

From all such practices Himmler stood rigidly aloof. He imbued his SS with the character of Teutonic Knights and forbade them, under

The idealist. To practice genocide is permissible, but not to enrich oneself as a consequence

penalty of death, ever to soil their hands 'with so much as a confiscated cigarette' if in the course of duty they were ever in a position to do so.

'He who robs a victim of a single pfennig shall die,' he said once in a speech to SS leaders. 'A certain number of SS men – not many – disobeyed this order and died without mercy. We had the moral right, we had the duty to our own people, to kill these people [the Jews] who wanted to kill us. But we have no right to enrich ourselves by a watch, a mark, a cigarette or anything else. I shall never stand by and watch the slightest rot develop or establish itself here. Wherever it forms we shall burn it out together. We can say we have performed this task [the destruction of the Jews] in love of our people. And we have suffered no damage from it in our inner self, in our soul, in our character.'

The chivalrous 'Order of Knighthood' with which Himmler invested his SS leaders was no mere abstraction. 'The SS represents racial purity,'

Himmler's folly, the 'medieval' Wewelsburg Castle, built to be a focus for his Knightly Order of SS leaders

he wrote. 'The leaders must be worthily taught the traditions of their predecessors.'

The predecessors he had in mind were the Knights of the Teutonic Order who in the 12th Century founded a hospital for Christians suffering the ravages of heathen Goths, then became a military company concerned to convert heathens into Christians – which as time went on they did more by brutality than by missionary zeal and combined their efforts with territorial conquests. The parallel between the medieval and modern forms of totalitarianism is obvious; but it was the symbols and ceremonies of the Order that appealed to Himmler. With Hitler's approval, obsequiously gained in a charade in which the chinless wonder of the Third Reich had an audience of the Führer wearing the white mantle of Grand Master, he caused to be built in Paderborn, Westphalia, a 'medieval' castle for the indoctrination of high-ranking SS officers in 'the spirit of Germany's past greatness now returning'. The castle cost 11,000,000 marks and Hitler indulged the whim rather as a reward for Himmler's ceaseless busyness and slavish devotion than for belief in, or

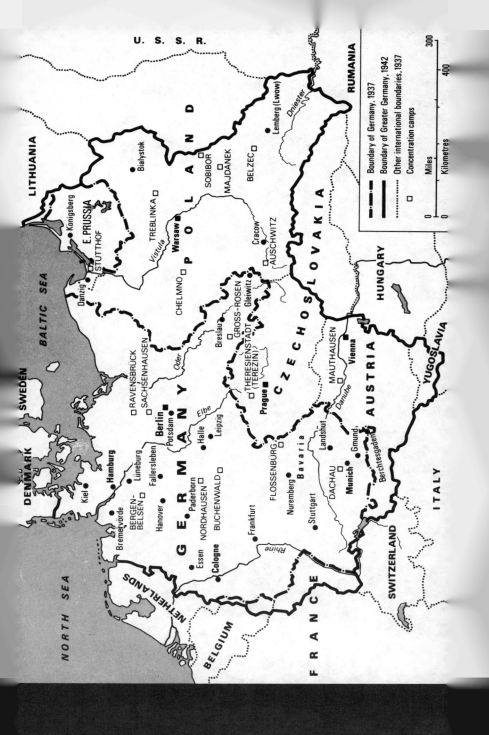

Himmler on his birthday with Wolff and Heydrich: the day of the Dachau tour

approval of, the tenets of the Order.

The building of Wewelsburg Castle was the only charge Himmler ever put upon the State. His house at Gmund he bought out of the proceeds of the sale of the Waltrudering farm, raising the small balance of the purchase price by a mortgage on which he willingly paid exorbitant interest. To pay interest was one of the obligations of every borrower and it must be done whether demanded or not. If he borrowed a cigar he repaid it punctiliously with a bigger cigar or a cigar-and-a-half; and when, as often happened, he found himself short of pocket money toward the end of the month and borrowed a mark or two from a colleague, he repaid it with scrupulously exact interest. He judged it proper to deny himself a bottle of wine during the next month to straighten his personal expenditure again.

This paragon of financial virtue, who kept his loose change in a grey leather purse as colourless as his personality, arranged a special treat for himself on his thirty-fifth birthday, 7th October 1935. He personally conducted a bevy of distinguished visitors – they included Rudolf Hess, Hitler's deputy and sometime secretary – on a tour of Dachau concentration camp.

He displayed with considerable pride the searchlights, electrical fences and gun emplacements designed to prevent escapes. ('The contractors told me that the voltage is 75,000 and the creature who touches the wires turns instantly to a blackened crust. It's a curious phenomenon.') By this time the Nuremberg Laws, promulgated three weeks previously, were beginning to have their effect on the intake of prisoners and consequently on the size of the camp staff. Eicke, the Commandant, whom Himmler followed at the respectful distance of two steps, led them to the new barracks and married quarters that were being built by the prisoners working under armed guard –'From 3 am to sunset in the summer months,' Eicke informed the Reichsführer and distinguished visitors, 'and from 4 am to sunset in the winter months. The barracks are scheduled for completion in January, the married quarters by the spring.'

There were, as Hess noted, no signs of brutality – but Himmler said in a regretful tone that sooner or later severity would have to be practised since scum of the earth such as came here could understand nothing else. It would be most distressing – though of course necessary – for the guards and their families to have to live so close to unpleasantness and indeed take part in it.

Himmler added to this ludicrously

Below: **Rudolf Hess, when conducted round Dachau, noted no signs of brutality. Himmler told him that, regretfully, stern measures would probably soon be necessary.** *Above right:* **SS officers visiting KZ Mauthausen.** *Below right:* **Vigilant** *Totenkopf* **(Deaths Head) guards at Mauthausen**

misplaced compassion the explanation that 'it is the tragedy of the élite to have to participate in acts of violence for the glory of the Fatherland.' He then went on to explain that his Totenkopf ['Death's Head'] units (this was the name he had given the SS men detailed for duty in concentration camps) had many compensations for their sacrifices. These 'compensations' included the privilege of listening to pre-breakfast lectures on the inspiring life of Adolf Hitler and readings from Rosenberg's *Myth of the Twentieth Century* and Darré's *Blood and Earth*. The Totenkampf guards'

wives and children above the age of two years were required to listen to these daily heart-lifting readings, which were followed by the regulation breakfast of porridge, Apollinaris mineral water (ownership of the Apollinaris company was part of the economic expansion of the Reich), leeks and herb tea compounded from a recipe of Marga Himmler's. Some of the SS wives suggested that porridge might make them fat, which was not in accordance with the Nazi-Nordic genetic pattern laid down by Himmler. But the Reichsführer assured them that they were mistaken in their

assumption. As proof he pointed to Anthony Eden and Nevile Henderson (at that time British Ambassador to Yugoslavia), who were both of slender build and came from the British aristocracy –'in which society nothing whatever is ever eaten for breakfast but porridge'. His researches must have been on a par with Heydrich's into the prevalence of spies in the population of Britain.

There was another great treat for the visitors on this birthday tour of Dachau. It was a dissertation by Himmler at lunchtime on the plans he had 'for the future of the German race'. These plans included the complete reorganisation of the physiognomy of the people 'on the basis of Mendel's Law'. This remarkable reorganisation, he claimed, would, 'by excluding undesirable elements in marriage partners and the selective breeding of a super race in conditions of chivalry and discipline, result in little more than a hundred years in an authentic German type that will be the mould for the future of civilisation.'

He was to pursue this lunatic notion doggedly for the rest of his life. Eight years later, at the height of the war, we find him loquaciously battering away at it to another group of distinguished visitors: 'One principle must be absolute for the SS man: we must be honest, decent, loyal and comradely to members of our own blood and to no-one else. What happens to the Russians, what happens to the Czechs, is a matter of utter indifference to me. Such good blood as there may be among the nations we shall acquire for ourselves, if necessary by taking away the children and bringing them up among us. Whether the other people live in comfort or perish of hunger interests me only in so far as we need them as slaves for our culture; apart

Neville Henderson, British Ambassador to Berlin, on his arrival. Himmler cited his slim figure as proof of the non-fattening properties of porridge

from that it does not interest me. Whether or not ten thousand Russian women collapse from exhaustion while digging a tank ditch interests me only in so far as the tank ditch is completed for Germany. It is a crime against our own blood to worry about them or assume they are human as we are human. Most of you know what it means to see a hundred corpses lying together – five hundred or a thousand – in Auschwitz, Ravensbrück, Lublin. . . . To have gone through this and yet to have remained decent, this has made us hard. This is a glorious page in our history.'

At the birthday luncheon at Dachau Himmler revealed other fascinating aspects of Germany's glorious history, past and present, as interpreted and studied by himself. As Grand Master of his Order of Teutonic Knights he had made the rule of having only twelve guests at his table 'like the British King Arthur, who was really a Teuton and copied the idea of his Round Table from the Court of Barbarossa'; he had instituted a method of thought compulsion' in which he and other Knights of the Order sat in one room and concentrated their wills on someone in the next room so that he was 'powerless to keep his secrets in the influence of knightly compulsion'; he had made some studies of theosophy and was of the opinion that he himself was a reincarnation of Heinrich I, founder of the First Reich in the early Middle Ages; and he had appointed several archaeological experts to make studies of the skulls of 'Jewish Bolshevik commissars and other sub-human species' – presumably so that nature might not make mistakes when turning out the future super-Teutons.

According to Hess, these projects and fantasies were taken seriously rather than indulgently, which is surprising. But it is probable that indoctrinated totalitarians found them easier to swallow. For, as Joachim Fest says, 'Crazy ideas of this sort exist on the lunatic fringe of

'It is a crime against our own blood to . . . assume they are human as we are human.' (Himmler)

every society in almost every epoch, exercising varying degrees of practical influence. Stable social orders absorb those who hold them relatively unharmed and allow them a certain limited field of activity as founders of sects, quack doctors or pamphleteers. It is only in a hopelessly disrupted society that a figure like Heinrich Himmler can acquire political influence; and only under a totalitarian form of government offering universal salvation could he come to hold the power that offered some prospect of putting his ideas into practice. His sobriety and apparent common sense, which deceived outsiders, were precisely what made his career possible [and enabled him to reach] the highest power, a calculating man of faith who without doubt or challenge trampled over millions, leaving behind him a trail of blood and tears, the most dreadful combination of crackpot and manipulator of power, of quack and inquisitor, that history has ever known. Concentration camps and herb gardens, such as he planted at Dachau and elsewhere: these are still the most apt symbols of his personality.'

Left: **The *Reichsführer-SS* indulges his knightly fantasy, saluting his supposed ancestor Heinrich I, first king of Germany.** *Below:* **Camp inspection at Buchenwald**

Alter ego and enemy

Heydrich and Himmler in relentless
pursuit of other people's weaknesses —
including each other's

Wallowing as he did increasingly in racial fantasies and glutinous compassion for the tribulations of his Totenkopf guards in the concentration camps, Himmler found considerably less time to devote to his industrious accumulation of information. His researches into the possibilities of human stud farms, legal polygamy, deportation of 'alien' elements in the Third Reich, and a crazy idea he had for the establishment of a racially and ideologically supreme SS State (it was to be in Burgundy) where would flourish 'the botanical garden of Germanic blood' occupied him unremittingly.

But on the score of time lost for assembling files on future victims of Reich tyranny he had no need to worry. His alter ego and votary, Heydrich, had from the first dedicated himself to the probing of secrets and the turning over of the pages of likely and unlikely subjects' lives. Just as Himmler had secured to himself the 'corrupt angel' of the Third Reich by holding over him the unspoken threat of revelation of his Jewish blood, so Heydrich went in relentless pursuit of knowledge of other people's weakness, believing that only such knowledge created power.

Personal power was Heydrich's absolute God. Hitler's megalomania involved the Utopian notion as the kingpin of a nation, a race, that would subjugate the world; Heydrich's, like that of some terrible Renaissance pope, involved nothing but personal supremacy. He thought contemptuously of Himmler's mad ideological theories but was perfectly willing to display approval of them as a means to his own ends – which were no less than ultimately to depose Hitler from

leadership and himself become Führer of the Third Reich.

With that objective hidden behind his cold pale eyes and thin lips, he avidly collected backstairs gossip about ministers, factory hands, servant girls, army generals. His ever-increasing band of agents brought him crumbs, gobbets, whole tomes of information. Nothing was too small, too large, too complex. Everything could be made to fit. As Hitler's plans worked themselves toward the climax of September 1939, Heydrich's network of spies of varying degrees of competence and reliability spread unhindered throughout Germany. Those caught in it could not be sure whether their nearest and dearest might not be secretly passing on the grist of past indiscretions to the SD mill. From the 'Night of the Long Knives' to the end of the war no life was free of suspicion or disentangled from the machin-

ations of Heydrich's SD – not even Hitler's. For Heydrich had personally amassed secret files of his own on the entire upper hierarchy of the Party.

This remarkable collection he kept in an armoured strongroom to which only he had the key. Hitler's file included evidence of the false award of his Iron Cross (it had apparently been awarded *after* the First World War, by Ludendorff, and its award backdated), and medical reports on treatment for his syphilis. Göring's sexual impotence, Robert Ley's non-Aryan genealogy, Daluege's record of mental instability, the criminal background of Martin Bormann (deputy Party leader), and Josef Goebbel's squalid love affair with the film actress Lida Barova, who was described as 'racially impure and sexually perverted,': these were all referred to in patiently accumulated notes, letters, photographs and recordings. Also, of vital value in

his relationship with Himmler was the evidence – recorded in letters and tape recordings taken via concealed microphones – that the Reichsführer-SS was supporting and giving protection to a Jewish cattle dealer named David Heymann, who had married the bastard daughter of Himmler's paternal uncle. (It was quite true.)

One of the means by which he obtained his information was by establishing, under State auspices, a glamorous brothel known as the Salon Kitty in one of the best residential suburbs of Berlin. To this, foreign diplomats, businessmen and high-ranking officers of the forces were invited. There were nine bedrooms bugged with microphones and concealed cameras and with all the apparatus of perversion readily available. Frau Kitty, the Madam, was a butcher's daughter from Munich, who was given an allowance of 15,000 marks

Left: Martin Bormann with Hitler. Bormann's criminal background was duly recorded and, with files on Hitler's syphilis and many more such dossiers, kept in Heydrich's armoured strongroom. *Below:* Robert Ley, like Heydrich himself, concealed a non-Aryan taint in his genealogy. *Right:* 'Madam' Kitty Schmidt, proprietress of the Salon Kitty – the brothel established by Heydrich in which every bedroom was bugged with cameras and microphones

a week to run the place luxuriously and pay the girls, who were never allowed out unless accompanied by a Gestapo shadow and were constantly under SD and medical supervision. (Any kind of venereal infection was spotted, and treated, immediately; but it was useful evidence for possible future blackmail of the infector.) Their only possible escape – and there is no evidence that any of them ever wanted to escape – would have been to concentration camps, since their heads were too stuffed with the confidences of State visitors – includ- ing those of Count Ciano, Mussolini's son-in-law, which proved extremely useful in furthering, in due course, the Axis alliance.

Heydrich himself was a regular patron – as he was of both topgrade and sleazy night clubs in Berlin. Aside from sports, in which he excelled and was always bitterly resentful if beaten, he found relaxation outside the domestic circle only in alcohol and sex. His womanising was straight-forward and violent. If the girls he fancied were uncooperative he could always persuade them by fear. Hey-

Below: **Count Ciano, Mussolini's son-in-law; a patron of the Salon Kitty.**
Above right: **A Berlin brothel in 1930.**
Below right: **A variety show of the kind Heydrich was addicted to**

drich and Gestapo were the cognomens of fear and became the most dreaded words in Germany. He had no difficulty in supplementing his undoubted attraction by coercion when necessary.

At home, on the rare occasions when he was there, his life was the life of any ordinary middle class family man. Lina had given him two sons and these he treated indulgently. He kept up the acquaintance with Canaris (who had come to think of him as 'despicable and dangerous') and still played chamber music with Frau Canaris when he had free weekends. On one

of these he revealed to Canaris the fissure with which his personality was riven.

They had set off back to Berlin together in Heydrich's official car at about ten o'clock on Sunday night, both with a heavy week's work ahead of them. Once in the city, however, Heydrich had turned his mind to a drinking spree and insisted on Canaris accompanying him into bar after bar.

'Gradually he became coldly and calculatingly drunk,' Canaris afterward recorded in his precise way. (He was now Hitler's Chief of Military Intelli-

gence.) 'He neither stumbled nor slurred his speech; but his eyes narrowed until they were almost invisible except as two pinpoints, and his lips twisted as if he were in the grip of an epileptic seizure. But paradoxically there was also in his manner a curious peace and relaxation, as if he had freed himself from some gripping pain and left only the visible manifestations of its torture on his features. At any moment, one thought, his contorted face would smooth out and reflect the calm the schnapps had induced. But it didn't. It was as if even in alcohol there was no final release for him.

'When we reached his flat he persuaded me –"commanded" is a better word – to go in for a final drink. I knew too much about his tainted blood to be fearful of him; but I humoured him because I was fascinated by the possible outcome of the evening.'

Canaris was not disappointed. As the two of them entered the flat and the light was switched on, Heydrich saw himself reflected in a full-length mirror on the wall opposite the door.

'He was swaying a little and I saw, rather than heard, his mouth twist into the words "filthy Jew". Then he snapped the Luger from its holster and fired three shots at the mirror.'

Splintering the mirror and obliterating the reflection in it was of course no means of releasing him from the tormenting presence of his tainted self. He was his own prisoner in a world in which the self-created chimeras of enmity could be endured only by the sadistic infliction of torture on others, with the justification of his secret fanatical demands for unlimited personal power to urge him on. But he was cunning enough to have kept himself and his ambition in the shadow of one who needed him. 'Destiny displayed remarkable perspicacity in bringing Heydrich together with the fussy, narrow-minded Himmler,' Fest comments. 'For Himmler's disastrous mixture of energy and dependence made him the ideal steward of other people's purposes . . . the

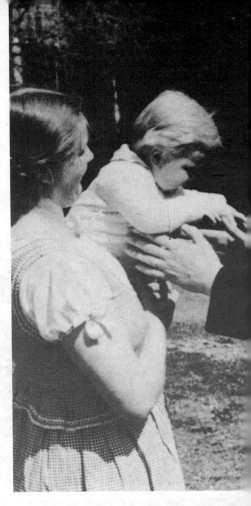

sinister features in his colourless philistine profile were lent by Heydrich . . . and each regarded the other as an instrument of his personal striving for power.'

Only enmity could ensue from this interdependence. It was an enmity that flared and died unpredictably. Sometimes it took the form of a mock obsequiousness on Heydrich's part, intended to torment Himmler for his sickening servility which he had intended to conceal with the pompous command to Heydrich that he and Lina were always to address him as Herr Reichsführer.

'Certainly, Herr Reichsführer, if

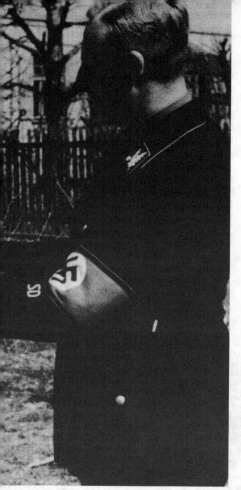

now indivisible. Personifications of mediocrity both, they saw greatness in each other just as they saw greatness in all the leaders and struggles of the Third Reich. But in making a funeral oration over the coffin of Heydrich after he had been assassinated in 1942, Himmler could find no more to say of him in general terms than that 'he was a man with an iron heart'; while in personal terms only meaningless schmaltz oozed from his lips: 'You, Reinhard Heydrich, have been a good SS man . . . I personally thank you for the unshakable loyalty and wonderful friendship which bound us in life and which death cannot break.'

Around Himmler and his entourage of thugs, Teutonic Knights, spies, theorists, civil, criminal, military and political police, hangers-on, agents, propagandists, indoctrinators and murderers, Europe headed rapidly for the war that Hitler made inevitable once he had dictatorial powers and found himself opposed mainly by pusillanimous statesmen and an unreasoning disbelief in his intentions.

None of the major moves toward war was made by Himmler or any of the organisations he directed with such skill. Regardless of the enormous power he wielded, he had no influence on Hitler and the Army Command. He would have dearly loved to have his fingers in the military pie, for he had never overcome his youthful devotion to the army with its routine, its orders and its hierarchy; and indeed in due course he was to persuade Hitler that he was suitable as an Army Commander – a lamentable mistake on the Führer's part; but for the time being, so far as his army ambitions were concerned he had to content himself with recruiting men to a special fighting branch of the SS. These Waffen SS divisions were to grow into some of the fiercest fighting units of the Wehrmacht. In instituting and fostering them Himmler completed the SS 'state within a state'. The Reichs-

that is the Herr Reichsführer's wish I will have the necessary arrangements made at once and report back to the Herr Reichsführer. Yes, certainly; yes, yes indeed, Herr Reichsführer!'

At other times Himmler, like a bullied child turning at bay, would, according to Lina, 'spit out vituperative words with all the venom of a snake':

'You and your logic! We hear about nothing but you and your logic! Everything I propose you batter down with your cold, rational criticism. I'm sickened to death by you and your logic.'

Enmity or no, the two men were

führer-SS was now in command of a freely moving wheel that duplicated all the machinery of the Reich itself – civil, political and military. With the SA reduced ignominiously to the tatters of a ragbag, its remnants nominally led by a one-eyed weakling called Viktor Luetze, whose efforts to revive it were hopeless, Himmler had no-one to throw sand in the cogs. His enterprises rolled smoothly toward the complete domination of Germany's internal affairs while Hitler himself relentlessly enmeshed the rest of the world.

The few years left before the darkening shadows of war fell across Europe were clearly signposted by the huge Party rallies at Nuremberg, where Hitler openly declared and displayed his intentions. Behind the thunder of tanks, artillery, and bombers whose construction he had referred to as 'part of the creation of work that forms the necessary economic recovery of the Reich,' the Führer justified his every action: withdrawal from the disarmament conference and

Waffen SS recruits in training

League of Nations, repudiation of the Locarno Pact, re-establishment of universal military service, the restoration of the 'unrestricted sovereignty of the Reich'. Soothingly he mitigated the driving forces of violence with the syrup of peace:

'I have no more fervent wish than everlasting peace for Germany and the world . . . I have re-established the Reich militarily only to make her a partner with equal rights.'

International reaction to such bland statements feebly displayed reassurance. The soporific effect of 'Herr Hitler's dissociation of his aims from the realms of conquest' (that was the London *Morning Post*) seemed to linger over, and undermine, the effect of a very different declaration: 'My educational principles are harsh. In his training schools for the Schutzstaffeln the Reichsführer-SS Himmler is hammering away at every weakness. He is bringing forth young men who will make the world tremble. I have demanded a violent, arrogant, fearless

Viktor Lutze, nominal head of the remains of the SA

Himmler's SS training schools were designed to produce 'young men who will make the world tremble'

youth. With them we shall create a new world. By the harshest tests they shall learn to master the fear of death. This is the stage of heroic young men.'

'If the rabbity-faced Himmler is bringing forth these rabbity litters of young men,' one sour reporter noted (and was expelled for it), 'there's considerable doubt about their rabbity qualities. They're violent and arrogant all right, and that isn't surprising.'

He had observed the results of the training Himmler had worked out for them in the early days, when there were a mere 300 *Ordnertruppen* who had to be worked up into the *corps d'élite* Hitler demanded.

Reveille at six am was followed by an hour's intensive physical training, the fifteen-minute breakfast of leek soup and porridge, an hour's weapon training, intensive study of the Führer's virtually unreadable *Mein Kampf* (in preparation for *viva voce* examinations that were given daily and had to be passed before the recruit was allowed out of barracks), and a 'hazard course' (rather similar to those undergone by the British Commandos) that would certainly involve river crossings, cliff climbings, battle with live ammunition, and some such test as standing to attention while a live hand grenade exploded on the recruit's helmet. Himmler noted that there was very little wastage of life in this last test, but that it 'showed up in true colours those who flinched and who had consequently to be turned down'. Heydrich invented another test that more frequently had gruesome results. This was for the recruit literally to 'dig for his life'. He was given a span of time – laid down in accordance with the nature of the ground – and in that time had to dig himself a hole in which he could be completely submerged. As the minutes flicked by and he plied his implements – these too varied according to the scaled severity of the test, and could be anything from a hand matchette to a pick – he was encouraged by the starting-up sounds of a nearby tank which, at the stop-watch signal of its commander, would drive straight for the wholly or partly submerged recruit and pass its track over his head if he hadn't dug himself in.

After the midday meal would come the barrack-square drill, 'which was worthy of a detention barracks or of Gibbon's description of Roman discipline: "the effusion of blood was the only circumstance which distinguished a field of battle from a field of exercise".' Then came the 'interior economy' – the preparation of barracks for inspection with every item of equipment scrubbed and polished and laid out in precise positions from which departure would ensure confinement to barracks or more serious punishment, scouring of floors and walls, and spot inspections of recreational literature. If this share of this ordeal was looked upon with favour 'the recruit could leave barracks if he was still capable of standing on his feet', as Reitlinger says. 'But he had to look as if he had just been unpacked to hang on a Christmas tree, incredibly pink, fresh and Teutonic, his well flattened pockets containing only a modest supply of paper currency which did not bulge, his paybook, his handkerchief creased according to regulation, and one prophylactic.' 'The prophylactic,' Himmler solemnly noted in one of his SS directives, 'is for protection only and is not intended to limit the number of times the recruit achieves congress with his chosen partner.' (Always supposing, presumably, that the recruit had the energy to achieve congress at all after the gruelling enterprises of the day.) But that was in the early days of SS training, when Himmler had not worked out his idealistic notions for the future of the great Germanic race. By the time he had done so another kind of congress had been achieved – the Anschluss with Austria in 1938, which was of course bloodless and, as Hitler delightedly pointed out, had the approval of 99.73 per cent of the Austrian population voting in a plebescite. (He mentioned nothing about the methods of the 'plebiscite'.) By 1938 few people in the Reich had doubts about the inevitability of war – a war, naturally, to maintain the 'unrestricted sovereignty of the Reich' which Hitler in his rantings edged with the trappings of his fervent wishes for everlasting peace; but which, whatever trappings it was edged with, would absorb men.

Into the arena of what might be called the perpetuation of the *corps d'élite* Himmler now stepped fully armed with his ideas of Teutonic Knighthood, plus suitable practical interpretations of them.

These included the Lebensborn ('Fount of Life'), an organisation dedicated to founding maternity homes for SS children orphaned by battle. Every SS man had deductions made from his pay to sponsor the upkeep of these homes, in case he himself might have his progeny cared for in one of them eventually. In

addressing SS men and pointing out their responsibility for ensuring the future of the Reich Himmler said: 'Only good blood, Nordic blood, can be considered. I said to myself that should I succeed in selecting as many men as possible from the German people, a majority of whom possess this valued blood, and teaching them military discipline and, in time, the understanding of the value of blood and the entire ideology that results from it, then it will be possible to create such an élite organisation which would successfully hold its own in all cases of emergency.'

Having stipulated his requirements rather as if he was ordering some new machinery, he went on to explain that in his researches into genetics and 'the marvellous authority of German folklore' he had discovered that children conceived in a graveyard were imbued with the spirit of 'all the dead heroes who lay therein.' SS men were, therefore, first of all encouraged to procreate before they set off for the battlefield, and, secondly, encouraged to conceive their children (presumably with Frauleins who had passed

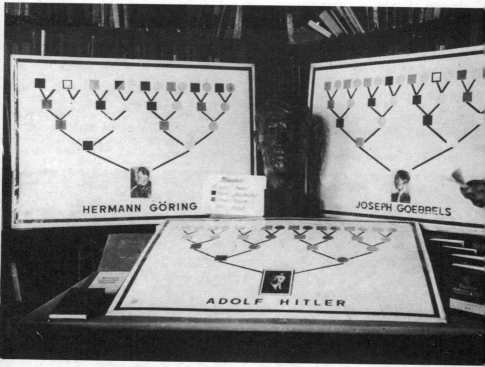

Above: The fanaticism of the Blood Purity mania. Charts show the unimpeachable heredity of Göring, Hitler and Goebbels. *Left:* German motorised police arrive to take over. *Far left:* The bloodless take-over of Austria in 1938. The Führer's cavalcade moves off from the stand outside the Vienna *Burgtheater*

the rigorous test of the SS marriage laws) on the uncomfortable bed of graveyard tombstones. Himmler specified the cemeteries that might be used for this unique kind of copulation – only those, naturally, where the deepest researches had revealed no traces of non-Nordic remains being buried. Lists of them were published regularly in the SS magazine *Das Schwarze Korps* – which, incidentally, was a tabloid journal founded and partly edited by Heydrich. As some acid English journalist pointed out, 'One might say that these lists give a new ring to the phrase "Poking about in graveyards", which hitherto has been reserved for the archaeologists.'

Das Schwarze Korps was the news medium for many other things besides the mating rendezvous of SS men. In 1936, for instance, when the Olympic Games were held in Germany, Heydrich published this cleverly restrained encouragement to visitors:

'For the first time since the advent of the Olympic Games Germany has the honour of being chosen as host to the nations. We should therefore like to make a point in passing: it is true that foreign tourist traffic is a commercial asset to any country; and the opinion may be current that these Olympic Games are welcomed principally in Germany because of the revenue brought in by the tourist traffic connected with the Games. But the man in the German street is not at all interested in the immediate turnover.

'We welcome you not as a foreign tourist but as one who comes to join hands with the Germans to pay tribute to the Greek ideal of bodily perfection.

'No-one will question you as to what political party or organisation you favour. Nobody will be interested in whether you are a Fascist, a member of a Liberal party, or from the Popular Front. The question does not affect the degree of kindness which the Germans will show you. On the other hand, as we do not interfere in

The 1936 Olympic games stadium

the internal problems of your country we take it for granted that you will accept the political conditions in Germany as they are and show them the same respect as we show yours.

'You will never be made to feel that we want to turn you into a National Socialist. National Socialism is an expression of the German spirit and therefore a national matter for ourselves alone. For this reason we do not invite criticism from people from abroad, just as we do not criticize affairs in their respective countries.

'But if you are really anxious to secure a better knowledge of National Socialism we shall help you to the best of our ability. You are quite free to use your own political judgement. But what you will see is not a carefully staged show but a natural crosssection of the German people.'

Printed in three languages – English, German and French – this quasitolerant plea for tolerance in others was successful not only in quietening the suspicions of large numbers of people who went to the Games simply as spectators, but also of gaining the interest of a number of men and women who subsequently became German agents in Britain and France. 'The visitations to the Salon Kitty were stepped up considerably during the Games', Willi Frischauer remarks in his biography of Himmler.

Many foreign journalists visiting the Games, particularly those from democratic countries, were interested in seeing the concentration camps – of which news had of course filtered out far beyond the bounds of Germany itself. They were blandly shown 'transit camps for political detainees and refugees awaiting emigration permits'. These were innocuous, well ordered, and apart from high wooden fences and guards at the gate scarcely prisons at all. The 'sights' shown did not of course include Dachau and its counterparts; but in 1936 even there it would have been difficult to observe anything but iron discipline and extremely hard work for the prisoners.

Saluting the German competitors

By 1938 the position was very different. That was the year of The Crystal Night or Night of Broken Glass, the climax of the Jewish pogrom which had begun with the promulgation of the Nuremberg Laws in 1935 and had increased with bitter intensity until, in October, Göring made a new order that in future all Jews must have their passports and other identity papers stamped with a large J. Simultaneously, by unhappy chance, the Polish government ordered the stamping of the passports of Poles living in Germany, and this order revealed the presence of some 20,000

Below: Identity card for Jews.
Above right: The anti-Jewish pogrom enters a new phase. The morning after the night devoted to the sport of smashing the windows of Jewish-owned businesses – the *Kristallnacht*.
Below right: A junior official at the German embassy in Paris is shot by a Polish Jew; the perfect excuse for intensifying the campaign against all Jews

Poles who had been living in Germany for more than five years. All these were arrested by the Gestapo and transported to the border; but there they were refused admission by the Polish government and in the following days were forced to camp in the No-Man's Land on the border in freezing weather and with no means of sustenance. One of the families who suffered there was named Grynspan. They were Polish Jews and they had a mentally unstable son, aged seventeen who lived in Paris. This boy, Herschel Grynspan, was understandably much affected by the well publicised news of the stateless people and determined to visit the German Embassy in Paris and make a protest. Unfortunately he bought a revolver first, and when he was taken to a junior official of the Embassy, Ernst von Rath, he simply shot him in the stomach. That was on 6th November. Two days later von Rath died.

The dead man had not been in any way anti-Semitic, and was in fact under surveillance from Heydrich's SD men for not being even a very good Nazi; but this of course made no difference. The incident was a perfect excuse for the formation of a new 'policy' determined on 'dealing with the Jewish question'.

An urgent telegram was sent from Himmler's Gestapo headquarters on the 9th November to all Gestapo command posts throughout Germany and Austria: 'Within a few hours action against Jews and particularly against synagogues is to begin. Nothing is to interfere with this action. Archives and property are to be safeguarded and will later be checked and confiscated by SD personnel. Preparations are to be made for the immediate arrest of from 20,000 to 30,000 Jews throughout the Reich. The Jews selected should be those with substantial property. Further orders will be transmitted during the night.'

A following telegram gave instructions to concentrate on 'male Jews in good health, who should be imprisoned

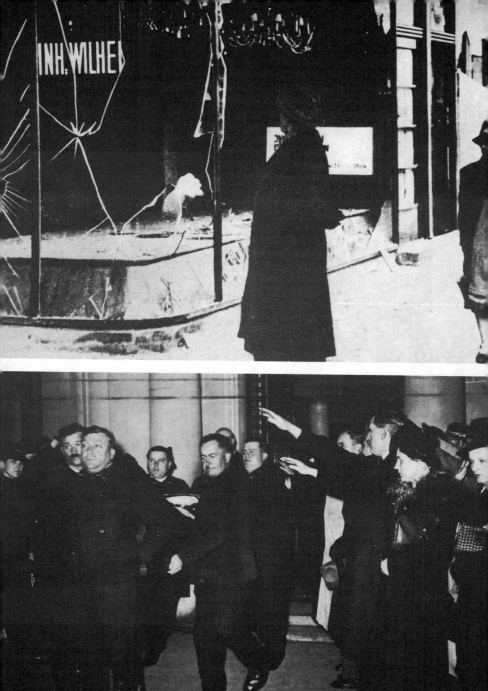

up to the capacity of the local jails and thereafter sent to concentration camps for internment.'

Throughout the night there was an orgy of looting, burning of buildings and stores, and deliberate smashing of windows of Jewish property. Some 815 stores were demolished by bomb and other explosions, and 200 warehouses and private houses set on fire. 20,000 Jews were arrested and thirty-six killed 'resisting arrest'.

Two days later a collective fine of 1,000,000,000 marks was imposed on the Jews of Germany and Austria for the destruction of the Crystal Night; all Jews were expelled from the schools, whether they were teachers or pupils; they were restricted as to the use of public transport, hospitals and shops;

Left: **The compulsory Star of David removes the last hope of anonymity.**
Below: **The round-up begins; prelude to the holocaust**

forced to wear the distinguishing badge of the Yellow Star of David, they would thereby attract to themselves the contumely of a nation that for some years had been conditioned in its hatred toward them; and Hitler in one of his most vitriolic speeches said, in part:

'Europe will not find peace until the Jewish problem has been settled. . . . If international Jewish financiers inside and outside Europe should again succeed in precipitating the nations into a world war the result will be the Bolshevisation of Europe and a victory for the Jews. . . . Either Europe and the world bow to my wishes and send all Jews to some desert island; or they try and resist me, in which case the accursed race will be annihilated.'

Heinrich Himmler, always the epitome of servility, reminded his Führer that all the apparatus to cope with the 'Jewish problem' was readily available and could be used on a much more in-

tensive scale than had thus far been approved 'on account of our over-merciful attitude to the scum-race'. He pointed out that though to date some 45,000 Jews had been legally expelled and 'rounded up,' only the very tip of the iceberg had been touched. 'The Jews permeate Europe like fog – they drift into smelly corners and make themselves invisible except for the miasma of their unclean presence.'

According to Albert Speer, who was present, he then 'virtually begged Hitler to place Jewish affairs entirely in his hands', giving as justification for his request the fact that Hermann Göring (who officially was Commissar for Jewish Affairs) now had the burden of the Luftwaffe on his shoulders and could ill afford the time 'for such an arduous task as ridding Europe of the Jews'.

Julius Streicher, Jew baiter

In this way Himmler wheedled into his own hands the task for which, by virtue of his years of academic study of race, blood and genetics he saw himself – quite genuinely – ideally fitted. Though it appears that Hitler had not shed his doubts about the viability of Himmler's cranky racial theories he had the evidence of the success of the SS and Gestapo to sway him. He gave in to the obsequious plea of the Reichsführer-SS. Himmler now as-

sumed the whip and reins of an apocalyptic horseman urging forward what he called, fancifully, 'the chariot of destruction'. The ground had been well prepared over the years by the propaganda of Dr Goebbels, the hideous Judæophobia of the perverted Gauleiter of Franconia, Julius Streicher, and the fortuitous murder of von Rath.

Even so, the new director of destruction was precluded by physical squeamishness, exemplified in the opening scene of this book and the ludicrous pity he displayed for the 'necessary' brutal activities of the concentration camp staffs, from steeping his own hands too deeply in Jewish blood. He therefore turned to Heydrich to 'expand and oversee the methods of the concentration camps'.

He could not have chosen anyone who took a more sinister delight in the possibilities opened up by Hitler's directive:

'In order to complete the mission imposed on you to solve the problem of the Jews by means of emigration, evacuation or destruction in the most suitable way in the circumstances leading to a possible solution, I herewith instruct you to make all the necessary organisational, practical and material preparations for a comprehensive solution of the Jewish question within the German area of influence in Europe. In so far as other central authorities are concerned they are to cooperate with you. I hereby instruct you further to submit to me as soon as possible a general plan with respect to organisational, practical and material means necessary for the execution of the desired Final Solution [*Endlösung*] of the Jewish question.'

It was Heydrich's mandate for mass murder; and his glee in planning the macabre details of gas chambers, crematoria, starvation, torture, sterilisation and forced labour was characteristically ghoulish. Here indeed was the ghastly grin of the angel of death on the other side of the colourless profile of Heinrich Himmler.

Operation Himmler

Poland invaded

In June 1939 Göring summoned Himmler to a meeting at which the general subject was preparation for imminent war and the particular subject the means by which the Allies could be provoked into making the first move – the Declaration. For it was no part of Hitler's schemes to fire the opening shot.

Himmler, with his normal servility, tinged since the days of his achievement of high power with pomposity, assured Göring that all the State services of which he had control were at the service of the Reich.

'Nothing could be more obvious,' Göring replied contemptuously. 'We are all at the service of the Führer and the Reich.' He went on to say that something more was needed than a reassurance that the Reichsführer-SS was at his desk doing his job: an actual plan, 'an idea for an incident, my dear Himmler, that will serve the purpose – something that is easily organised and absolutely foolproof, and does not involve suspicious numbers of men.'

Goebbels, who was present at the meeting, noted that Himmler immediately produced from his brief-case a file that had been prepared at the time of Hitler's seizure of Czechoslovakia Goebbels continues, 'that whatever plan was made, it must lend itself to successful propaganda – otherwise Germany would appear as the provoking country.'

With the typical vainglory of the small man puffed large with authority Himmler insisted, first, that the plan should be named after him. This concession granted – more from motives of propitiation than conviction – Himmler then departed for a consultation with Heydrich, upon whom he had become increasingly dependent for the construction of plots as distinct from

The Gleiwitz radio station, near the Polish border, scene of Operation Himmler, the faked incident which provided the excuse to attack Poland

the building and launching of grandiose Teutonic soap operas.

The plan as worked out and approved – enthusiastically – by Hitler was revealed in detail at the Nuremberg Trials by Alfred Naujocks, an SS veteran who had been seconded to the SD. Naujocks said: 'On or about 10th August 1939 Heydrich personally ordered me to stage a fake attack on the radio station at Gleiwitz [near the Polish border] and to make it appear that the attacking force was Polish. Heydrich said: "Practical proof is needed of these attacks by the Poles for the foreign press and for German propaganda." My instructions were to seize the radio station and to hold it long enough to permit a Polish-speaking German, who would be put at my disposal, to broadcast an anti-Hitler speech in Polish. Meanwhile, a dozen concentration camp inmates dressed in Polish uniforms were to be given fatal injections by a doctor employed by Heydrich, brought to Glei-

'In the very face of the Führer's appeals, Poland has chosen War.' (Voelkischer Beobachter)

witz and left dead on the ground near the radio station after being shot in a convincing way – I mean that their wounds must appear bloody – in order to prove that they had been shot while attacking. After the incident members of the press were to be taken to the spot so that they could photograph the so-called Poles so that they could appear in a press story in proof of Polish aggression.'

Though this Himmler-Heydrich plot was at one time rendered almost inoperable by the mundane detail of the difficulty of obtaining Polish uniforms – it was learnt eventually that Canaris, head of Military Intelligence, had a stock and these were the ones used – it was set in motion at noon on 31st August by the receipt of the code word and completed at eight o'clock that night. In the *Völkischer Beobachter* next day it was reported:

'A troop of Polish insurgents last night rushed into the building of Radio Gleiwitz. At that time only a skeleton staff was on duty. It is evident that Polish aggressors had exceptional knowledge of the station. They struck down staff and stormed the studio,

beating up the personnel with sticks and clubs.

'The raiders then read over the air a previously prepared propaganda speech in Polish and German. They stated that the town and radio station were in Polish hands and concluded with disgraceful abuse of the Führer.'

At daybreak, several hours before the *Beobachter* was on sale, the German armies, lined up and ready to move, poured across the Polish frontier and converged on Warsaw from the north, south and west.

'In the very face of the Führer's appeals,' the next editions said, 'Poland has chosen war.'

'A stupendous day for me,' Himmler wrote in his journal. 'Operation Himmler has served the Führer exactly to his requirements. I shall always be able to look back with pride to my conception and its success.' He failed to note, of course, that it was Heydrich who had worked out the details. Harbouring a continual resentment that in spite of his wide and terrible powers he had contributed none of the major moves toward war, he felt now that he had achieved the one move that had set the machinery of war in motion and that therefore his importance was supreme. According to his secretary, with whom he had formed a discreet sexual alliance, Heydrich visited him that day and remained coldly cynical 'in his careful disregard of his own part in the planning of Operation Himmler. He knew perfectly well that Heini would feel his inferiority all the more intensely if he acted that way.'

As Manvell and Fraenkel agree, 'Himmler's relationship with Heydrich during the first year of the war became deeply involved. When Himmler had first appointed Heydrich to the SS, they had both been young men, Himmler thirty-one years old and Heydrich twenty-seven. Even now, at the beginning of the war, Himmler was still not yet forty and Heydrich thirty-five. The closer observers of these two very different men ... differ very little in their assessment of Heydrich. Himmler was a mediocrity in comparison with Heydrich, who had little use for his commander's obsessions,

The Luftwaffe over Warsaw

racial or otherwise, and rapidly learnt how to exploit the power delegated to him. In the end . . . he undermined Himmler's position to such an extent that he achieved direct access to Hitler and, had he lived, might well in 1943 have been appointed Minister of the Interior by the Führer in order to break, or counterbalance, the power accumulated by Himmler. However, Heydrich's position in relation to Himmler was weakened, not strengthened, when in September 1941 Hitler, without consulting Himmler, appointed him Deputy Reich Protector in Czechoslovakia.'

The appointment was made because the then 'Protector', von Neurath, was weak, sick, and 'inefficient' and there were signs of considerable trouble from the Czech resistance movement. As Hitler saw, a very firm hand would be needed to put down a possible insurrection at a time when the *Barbarossa* operation to conquer Russia

Himmler talks with the Reich Protector of Czechoslovakia, von Neurath. In September 1941 Hitler appointed Heydrich Deputy Protector

had just begun and he could ill afford to weaken the Eastern Front by withdrawing troops for a minor operation in Czechoslovakia.

'Himmler has already magnetised to himself as much power as he can manage,' Hitler told Göring. 'Heydrich is more ruthless and less concerned with theoretical matters. He will do well there.'

As has been said, his mandate for murder was one he relished; but he saw it as a pleasure that should be relished for a considerable time. It could be made to do so by only very gradually 'selecting' those who were of Jewish or Slav race and therefore suitable only for deportation, sterilisation, or the gas chamber. The SS and the SD could be relied upon to, as it were, deliver them to him for 'trial' in numbers small enough to give him daily delight for as long as he cared.

There was not only the matter of his personal pleasure to be considered, however: the great Skoda armaments works was an essential part of the Reich war effort and had to be kept going at full power. Workers taken from there would have to be replaced.

To increase the difficulty, the resistance movement was very strongly concentrated there. Heydrich ingeniously overcame these snags by increasing all armaments workers' meat and fat rations, in order to, as he hoped, lessen the power of the resistance movement and allay suspicions as to his intentions. He then moved in what he described as 'X-ray units' which purported to make analyses of diets but which were in fact staffed by SD men going about their usual business as information gatherers. As might have been expected, they gathered all the appropriate information. For the time being it was used very carefully. A few Generals of the resistance were arrested, tried by drumhead court-martial and shot; then a brief spell of tranquillity was allowed to prevail, as if all the stern measures that were to be taken had been completed. Then, between the end of October and the beginning of December, Heydrich announced that all Jews in Bohemia and Moravia (as Hitler had now renamed the Czechoslovak Protectorate) would be deported 'to the East' and meanwhile would be concentrated in a 'transit camp' at Theresienstadt.

This caused the resistance movement to renew its activities. Armaments works began to suffer temporary 'breakdowns' due to unexplained faults in the machinery, minor explosions, and mysterious mistakes in blueprints and tool patterns. There were delays to trains arriving with supplies for the occupation troops. There was one 'accident' in which an SS man was injured when a broken piece of cornice fell from a shop gable.

Things had now gone far enough. Heydrich summoned one of his most efficient top-ranking SS men, Obergruppenführer Schacht-Isserlis, and handed over 100 dossiers on those whom the Gestapo and SD had investigated since Hitler's invasion of Czechoslovakia. 'There will be enough here to make an example,' Heydrich told him. 'A public execution . . . the square in front of the cathedral, I think. The Reichsführer-SS will at-

Frank, Himmler, Wolff and Heydrich in Prague

tend. He's a little squeamish at the sight of blood.' Schacht-Isserlis's notes recorded that Heydrich's eyes gleamed 'with a terrible iciness'.

The execution was but the opening phase of the wave of terror that now swept through Prague – and indeed throughout Bohemia-Moravia – at Heydrich's instigation. It was his mad policy, declared to Hitler, completely to exterminate the 30,000,000 Slavs and Jews of Eastern Europe: 'There will be plenty of room for them in Russia as the Russian lands fall to the Wehrmacht,' he said blandly, but extermination, not deportation, was his true plan. The crematoria at Theresienstadt, ostensibly a camp for aged and 'privileged' Jews (that is, those who had sufficient money and property to buy themselves the privilege of living in a ghetto and being starved to death or finding themselves the subjects of Heydrich's 'euthanasia' programme) continually belched forth the smoke of murdered bodies. The trains departed for Auschwitz and Belsen and Dachau and the rest, stuffed with scarcely living bodies; the mass graves were dug by the victims themselves and the machine-guns swept them downward; the SS guards looked on grimly and, with typical German efficiency ordered 'a few more shootings' if the graves still appeared to have room in them. The more refined experiments 'for the benefit of science' were still to come, as were the mass exterminations by Zyklon B and injections of bacteria; but there was no shortage of material for the Eichmanns of the Reich and the Totenkampf guards.

In Heydrich's Protectorate, where he had the absolute power of the Führer's viceroyalty, the hostility grew – as was inevitable in a conquered country; but naturally with the utmost secrecy. Controlled from London now, the Czech resistance movement decided that Heydrich must be assassinated. Two Czech volunteers, Jan Kubis and Josef Gabcik, were given Commando training

in Britain and dropped by parachute near Prague at the beginning of 1942. The Gestapo were well aware of their arrival, but not of their purpose; and for this reason Himmler ordered that they should not be arrested until that purpose had been revealed. Given time, Himmler felt sure, they could be trapped in their designs and would thereby prove more useful than if they were set upon at once.

But for once the Gestapo delayed too long; and Kubis and Gabcik were too well aware of the need for discretion to allow their plans to seep out of their own knowledge. They met rarely, avoided every possibility of

The Czech volunteers Jan Kubris (above) and Josef Gabcik (below), trained in Britain to be Heydrich's assassins. *Right:* Heydrich, the 'Butcher of Prague', enjoys the circus at the height of the terror for which he was responsible

being overheard or watched, and committed nothing to paper. Thus it took them several months to bring their plan to fruition. But by the end of May it was ready.

It was also very simple. Heydrich was commuting fairly regularly to Berlin by plane and was always driven to the airport by the same route – one that involved a sharp descent from the city to the River Vltava and the negotiation of a sixty-degree hairpin bend at the approach to the bridge over the river. At the bend his car was forced to slow to walking pace and there was little chance of a skilled marksman with a Sten gun missing him. . . . The chance was covered, however. If Gabcik failed with his Sten, Kubis had a hand grenade. Also, from the point of view of detection the site was ideal. Many tramlines converged on the junction and the bend and there were always groups of people waiting to cross. It was reasonably certain that few of them, seeing the assassination of Heydrich, would make much effort to apprehend the assassins. His grim sobriquet, The Butcher of Prague, had become firmly attached to him in a whispering campaign of hatred.

On 27th May, after three days of patient attendance on the corner,

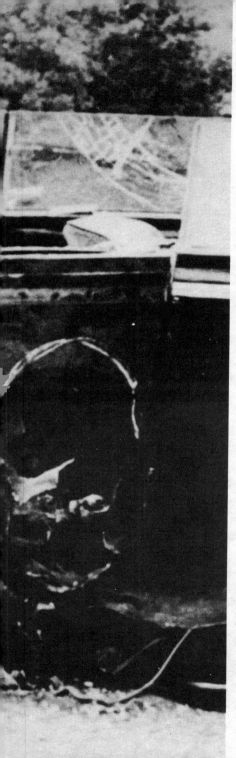

The Protector's Mercedes after the grenade attack which fatally wounded him

Kubis and Gabcik were rewarded.

'Heydrich had no fear of physical attack,' his biographer says. 'Throughout all the years he had been head of the Gestapo and SD he had been confident in the ability of the secret police to keep him immune from danger. As Reich Protector his indifference to the threat of assassination remained. He was openly contemptuous of the "bourgeois Czechs who hadn't enough guts to do anything". In the face of constant warnings from his subordinates he persisted in acting more like a popular matinée idol than the German Protector on whom the whole hate of the Czech nation was concentrated. His SS bodyguard irritated him and security precautions were things to be flouted. While Hitler, Göring and – above all – Himmler, travelled everywhere in armoured limousines with four-ply bulletproof glass, Heydrich, as often as the weather permitted, drove through Prague in the front seat of an open three-and-a-half litre Mercedes convertible. He had no protection beyond the side-arms carried by himself and his trusted chauffeur, Oberscharführer Klein.'

Therefore when Kubis and Gabcik saw the green Mercedes descending the hill and slowing for the hairpin bend they knew they had nothing to fear from outriders. As the car swung slowly level with him, Gabcik raised the Sten from under the raincoat that, draped across his elbow, had been concealing it. But by the irony of fate, with Heydrich's narrow eyes already in his sights, Gabcik's gun, inexplicably jammed, failed to fire. Also, Heydrich had spotted him and now screamed to Klein to stop as he freed the revolver from the holster at his belt. The car skidded and passed Kubis, who automatically reacted to Gabcik's failure by hurling his grenade.

It exploded with a violent flash against the door of the car at the very moment when Heydrich was leaping from the car in pursuit of Gabcik, who was now fleeing across the junction between trams that had halted in the confusion caused by the explosion. But Heydrich had leapt slightly too late. He suddenly turned from the pur-

suit and staggered back to the wrecked car with blood spreading across the black and silver uniform and dripping on to the road. No-one in the quickly gathering crowd made any move to help. Hitler's Viceroy was a man for whom no compassion existed even in the extremity of death.

After some delay two SS men ap-

peared on the scene and together with Klein they got Heydrich into the back of a baker's cart, where he lay among sacks of flour and cartons of cooking fat and was taken to the Bulovka hospital. He died eight days later from blood poisoning caused by irremovable particles of leather, steel and horsehair from the upholstery that had been

Above: Himmler at Heydrich's grave; a touching scene. *Above left:* The paratroopers' bodies in front of the church where they had been hiding. *Left:* The dreadful vengeance. The bodies of the men of Lidice

forced into his spleen when the grenade exploded.

There were of course immediate reprisals. Hostages were rounded up indiscriminately and shot. A reward of 1,000,000 Czech crowns was offered for the capture of the assassins – both of whom had escaped to hiding in the crypt of the Greek Orthodox Church. They remained there safely for nearly three weeks, during which time they were kept alive with food brought to them by members of the resistance. It was almost inevitable that the Gestapo should find somebody who could be tortured into the revelation of their hiding place. They were shot by the SS on 18th June 1942.

But that was not enough. The day after Heydrich's state funeral at which Himmler made his turgid oration over the gun carriage, the village of Lidice, north-west of Prague, was completely destroyed on Hitler's personal order. Every brick and stone in it was razed to the ground. The entire male population was shot, the women sent to concentration camps for sterilisation and 'medical experiments'. The children – ninety of them – were dragged from their mothers and despatched to concentration camps from which only seven were known to have emerged at the end of the war.

Walter Schellenberg, the head of the Foreign Intelligence section (Amt VI) of Heydrich's SD, said after he was released from jail in 1950 that two months after Heydrich's death Himmler was consulting with him in his Berlin office. Heydrich's deathmask was on the wall beside his immense desk with its perfectly ordered and docketed folders and indexes.

'He was indeed a man with an iron heart,' Himmler said. 'And at the height of his power fate purposefully took him away.' There was, says Schellenberg, an unmistakable emphasis on the word 'purposefully'. 'Then he nodded his head in approval of his own words and his small cold eyes glinted behind their pince-nez like the eyes of a basilisk.'

Operation cyanide

One small incident in the Final
Solution

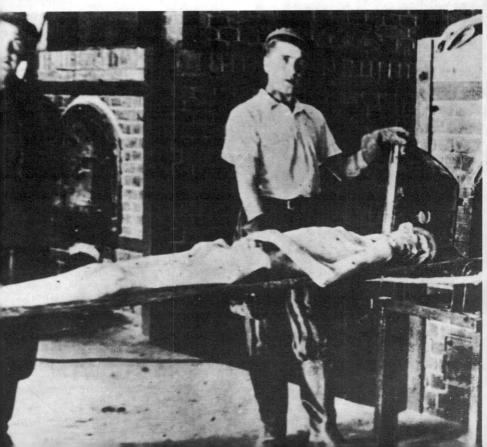

Though freed from Heydrich's rivalry and domination it appears that Himmler absorbed, as though by some curious process of osmosis, all the younger man's obsessional hatred of Jews. He no longer displayed his attitude of cold detachment. True, his frenzied dedication to myths, folklore, and the Utopian notion of a Teutonic race who would dominate the world continued. But rather as if he had taken to himself the sinister mask of his alter ego and was imbued by some residue of Heydrich's spirit, he pursued with a new viciousness the destruction of the abominated race.

Almost as soon as Heydrich's body had been buried in Invaliden cemetery, Berlin, he sent out an order for the 'resettlement' in concentration camps of all the Polish Jews in the Warsaw Ghetto – a walled city in which Hey-

drich had accumulated some 400,000 Jews with the object of starving them out.

'I decided to destroy this entire Jewish residential area,' Himmler said himself in a speech to SS men that was preserved with hundreds of others in his meticulous way and read in evidence at the Nuremberg Trials, 'by setting every block on fire, including the blocks of residential buildings near the armament works. One block after another was systematically evacuated and subsequently destroyed by fire. The Jews then emerged from their hiding places and dugouts in almost every case. Not infrequently, the Jews stayed in the burning buildings until, because of the heat and fear

A commonplace sight in the Warsaw Ghetto

of being burned alive, they preferred to jump down from the upper storeys after having thrown mattresses and other upholstered articles into the street. With their bones broken, they still tried to crawl across the street into blocks of buildings which had not yet been set on fire or were only partly in flames. Some of the Jews changed their hiding places during the night, by moving into the ruins of burnt-out buildings, taking refuge there until they were found by our patrols. Their stay in the sewers also ceased to be pleasant after the first week. Frequently we could hear from the street loud voices coming through the sewer shafts. Then the men from the Waffen-SS, the police or Wehrmacht engineers courageously climbed down the shafts to bring out the Jews and not infrequently they stumbled over Jews already dead, or were shot at. It was always necessary to use smoke bombs to drive out the Jews. Thus one day we opened 183 sewer entrance holes and at a fixed time lowered smoke bombs into them, with the result that they fled from what they believed to be gas to the centre of the former ghetto, where they could then be pulled out of the sewer holes. A great number of Jews, who could not be counted, were exterminated by blowing up sewers and dugouts.'

That summer of 1942 was one of maniacal activity for Himmler. His special armoured train went west, north and south, ever in search of fuel for his crematoria and 'fertiliser for the herb gardens of the future Greater German Reich.'

At Auschwitz, according to Höss, who accompanied him, 'He watched with interest the complete routine of destruction of a transport of Jews that had just arrived. They were taken to a decontamination centre and told to undress to be disinfected; which they did – men, women and children alike. Then they were all sealed into a gas chamber and killed. We were given

dinner that night at the home of the local Gauleiter. I remember telling Himmler some of my camp guards were very inefficient. He replied that I must use more dogs. Next day we returned to the camp and he watched, unemotionally, while naked women prisoners were whipped for disobedience. He had in fact ordered intensified beatings of undisciplined prisoners. The beatings were given on the naked buttocks of male and female alike, their bodies were strapped down on wooden racks. I do not think Himmler gained any perverted sexual enjoyment from this. He watched rather sadly, as if he bore a great weight of responsibility.'

As the war went on and Germany began to meet her early reverses, on the Eastern Front, in North Africa and Italy, the problem of shortage of labour naturally became increasingly difficult to solve. Himmler then turned his attention to a plan for 'The Delivery of Anti-social Elements to the Reichsführer-SS to be Worked to Death'. Road construction, rebuilding, the burying of the dead in bombed cities, and similar projects demanding large labour forces were now fed by 'privileged' prisoners from the concentration camps. Their 'privilege' was solely and simply to work until they fell dead from exhaustion and starvation. Noting in the documentary returns that reached his desk daily that in a single month 250,000 Jews had been thus exterminated Himmler made a note in the file that they had 'died for the greater glory of the German Reich'. The file closed, he turned to his secretary and instructed her to send to Auschwitz 1,000 toy balloons which had been indented for by one of the most infamous of the camp guards, Oswald Kaduk. Kaduk's satanic ploy was to issue the balloons to incoming children before they were led away to the medical rooms to be injected with phenol at the rate of ten a minute. Fond in an indulgent way of his own children – including those he had by his secretary-mistress

Hedwig – Himmler apparently believed that it was a sort of *pourboire* that would give children pleasure and prepare them for the pumping of phenol into their hearts. 'They die for the Führer' was one of his inconsequential remarks to his physiotherapist Felix Kersten. 'He said it as casually as a dog-loving Englishman makes his little dog roll over and "die for the king"', Kersten records.

Kersten occupied the unique position in Himmler's life of being able to wring from him concessions to individual victims of Hitler's Final Solution as the price of the relief he was able to give the Reichsführer-SS with his massage. The spasms of colic from which he suffered brought agonising pain for perhaps five days at a time, and only Kersten was able to help him. In exchange Kersten wheedled promises from Himmler and even got him to sign letters authorising the release of victims already on their way to the concentration camps. It was a laudable blackmail and Himmler wryly observed, 'The good doctor Kersten massages a life out of me every time he comes.'

But no-one could relieve the insanity of a mind that for the greater part of forty-five years had ploughed the furrow of complete servility to the

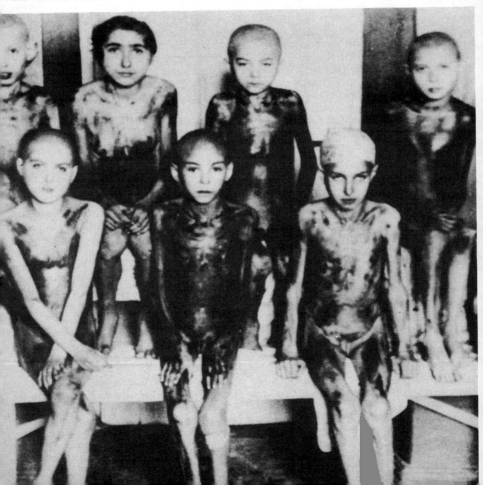

Warsaw Ghetto children sit for their portraits before being murdered. 'They die for the Führer'

mad idealism of establishing a super-race. If the devoutly exaggerated completeness of his loyalty to the Führer-God corresponded to a deep need on his part for security and 'something to hold on to', it is also obvious that his faith barely stood up to the final fall of the Third Reich. For when, with the turn of the tide in the war and Hitler's ever more obvious failure, the first cracks appeared in the feet of the clay, he instantly relapsed into the insecurity that was the basis of his character. It may be taken as proved – on the fairly extensive evidence available – that from 1943 onwards he had contact with the growing but still feeble resistance movement in Germany. There is little doubt that he played some part in the July plot against Hitler's life, for it is scarcely believable that the head of a secret police organisation with ramifications as wide as those of the Gestapo could not have moved more quickly and more effectively against the conspirators.

'Fate,' says Kersten, 'gave Himmler a position that he was incapable of managing. There was something spasmodic in everything he did. There was a dichotomy in his nature. It was fundamental. His own character was

The slightly injured Führer walks from the scene of his attempted assassination with Bormann, Göring and Keitel

weak and he preached toughness. He
carried out actions that were quite
foreign to his nature because he made
a god of servility and his Führer
ordered them. He extended this even
to the annihilation of human beings.
Though he had the mind of an ordinary clerk or schoolmaster he was
dominated by another Himmler whose
imagination was controlled by such
phrases as "The preservation of the
Germanic race justifies cruelty", or
"Unqualified obedience to the Führer". This other Himmler entered
realms which transcended the merely
human and entered into another
world.'

Himmler entered literally into another realm, the realm of death, on
23rd May 1945. Hitler was dead, the
war was over, the Reichsführer-SS
had received his formal dismissal
from Hitler's successor, Admiral
Dönitz:

'Dear Herr Reichsführer, In view of
the present situation I have decided to
dispense with your further assistance
as Reich Minister of the Interior and
member of the Reich Government, as
Commander-in-Chief of the Reserve
Army, and as Chief of the Police. I
now regard all your offices as abolished.
I thank you for the services which you
have given to the Reich.'

That was on 6th May. Two days
later, at midnight, the war officially
ended. For two weeks Himmler and a
small and irresolute entourage tramp-
ed about a hundred miles, vaguely and
senselessly in the direction of the
Elbe and Luneburg Heath, where on
4th May the German surrender had
been signed at Montgomery's headquarters. His intention must have
been to escape, since he had shaved
off his moustache, abandoned his
pince-nez, and adopted the thin but
theatrical disguise of a black eye-
patch – perhaps with some inner
desperate need to draw attention to
himself even at the price of capture.

Together with a number of other
suspects he was rounded up at Bremer-
vörde, where there was a check-point,

and taken to 031 Civilian Interrogation Camp, Luneburg. At four o'clock in the afternoon he was paraded before the officer in charge, Captain Tom Selvester, who afterward recorded:

'The first man to enter my office was small, ill-looking and shabbily dressed, but he was immediately followed by two other men, both of whom were tall and soldierly-looking, one slim and one well-built. The well-built man walked with a limp. I sensed something unusual, and ordered one of my sergeants to place the two men in close custody, and not allow anyone to speak to them without my authority. They were then removed from my office, whereupon the small man, who was wearing a black patch over his left eye, removed the patch and put on a

Left: Admiral Dönitz, Hitler's successor, leaves his quarters in Flensburg in May 1945. *Below:* The body of *Reichsführer-SS* Heinrich Himmler; born 1900, died by his own hand 1945. Unmourned

pair of spectacles. His identity was at once obvious and he said "Heinrich Himmler" in a very quiet voice.'

He was stripped and searched for concealed poison phials; but nothing was found. He had concealed a capsule of cyanide between two of his teeth. While being more thoroughly examined by a doctor who suspected that the black projection in his mouth was not a carious tooth he bit down on the capsule and swallowed the cyanide. For fifteen minutes or so there were frantic efforts to save his life by the use of stomach pumps and artificial respiration. But they were unavailing. Reichsführer-SS Heinrich Himmler had tricked his captors.

Two death-masks were taken. The first shows his features twisted by the contortions of agony into a monumental expression of diabolical evil; in the other he is relaxed, peaceful, displaying the face of an ordinary suburban commuter with a nine-to-five job and a lawn to mow on Saturday afternoons.

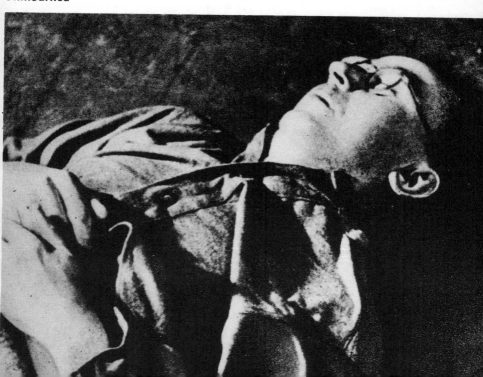